PERSPECTIVES AND PRINCIPLES:

A College Administrator's Guide to Staying Out of Court

by Dennis R. Black, J.D.
and Matt Gilson, J.D.

Edited by Matt Gilson, J.D.

Compiled and updated from material which first appeared in
PERSPECTIVE: The Campus Legal Monthly

Magna Publications, Inc.
2718 Dryden Drive
Madison, Wisconsin 53704

Copyright © 1988 by Magna Publications, Inc., 2718 Dryden Drive, Madison, Wisconsin 53704. All rights reserved. No part of this book may be reproduced in any form or by any means without permission in writing from the publisher.

Printed in the United States of America

ISBN 0-912150-07-6 $77.00

Contents

Introduction

If You Even Think You're Going to Be Sued ...

Once someone actually files a lawsuit against a college or student organization, the scrambling begins.

Decisions have to be made quickly. The adverse effects of the lawsuit need to be evaluated, arrangements for counsel must be made, alternatives to litigation should be considered, and, finally, the group sued needs to decide whether to contest the matter or not. These considerations all occur outside of the courtroom, but they have serious implications for anyone involved in a legal action.

FIRST QUESTIONS

Any lawsuit can prove time-consuming and costly. In addition to actual dollars and actual hours spent fighting it, the indirect, negative effect that a lawsuit can have on a school's operations, policies, and reputation can be costly in less quantifiable ways. Unfortunately, litigating a case on principle or even on the basis of a good defense may not be worthwhile.

Sometimes, suits must be regarded as a nuisance. Negotiating a nominal settlement may prove wiser than using more valuable resources fighting it out in court.

As soon as an organization or campus suspects that it may be sued, it should move to protect itself by arranging for quality legal counsel and adequately preparing for a defense. Underestimating the seriousness of a lawsuit can cause delay and weaken a case.

WHEN TO USE OUTSIDE COUNSEL

University counsel or staff may not always be suitable to defend every case. Outside counsel may be needed for cases involving specialized fields. When selecting outside counsel, consider the following:

- Does the attorney have any indirect contacts that could help the case?
- What is his reputation in the field?
- How many similar cases has he handled?
- How many have been won or lost?
- Does the attorney appear to be too rigid?
- Does he show a reluctance to settle?
- Will the attorney give the case all the attention it needs, or is he "spread too thin"?
- Are back-up attorneys and staff competent?
- What type of fee arrangements are offered?
- Is the attorney well-versed in the appropriate area of law?
- Is the attorney sympathetic to the campus position?

An experienced and knowledgeable attorney, on staff or on retainer, can develop strategy and make an educated guess about the case outcome. One consideration should always be an out-of-court settlement.

OUT-OF-COURT SETTLEMENTS

Some alternatives to litigation include negotiation by the parties, agreement between involved attorneys, and arbitration. In conflict resolution, involving legal and everyday issues, direct contact between the parties can lead to a fair arrangement acceptable to everyone. This strategy permits differences of opinion to be expressed and problems solved before positions harden in court. In fact, opposing parties may be able to clear up their misunderstandings and reach a reasonable settlement that makes more sense than a court-imposed judgment.

Disputes between a student and a school, or between an employee and a school, should first be negotiated in an informal atmosphere. All issues and concerns should be "put on the table" for open discussion. This process allows for all parties to understand both weak and strong positions, and helps to identify common ground for agreement. If a hostile environment has been created during a dispute, a respected "outsider" should be asked to sit in. Sometimes, an outsider can more easily identify areas for agreement and come up with innovative ideas.

If the actual parties to a suit cannot resolve the issues outside of the courts, perhaps their attorneys can. At any rate, try direct attorney agreement in order to speed up the whole process and eliminate court costs.

Arbitration uses a third party chosen to settle a dispute. Since all parties must agree on the choice of an arbitrator, there is common agreement that a settlement can work. Arbitrators are generally experts in specialized areas who have an understanding of issues that might be difficult to develop before a judge or jury. An arbitrator can bring out points the parties may not see, and may think of solutions they've overlooked. The American Arbitration Association is a well-established resource for procedures of this type.

The decision to negotiate a settlement or fight an issue out in the courts is rarely an easy one to make. A school may decide to litigate a case to protect a particular policy, such as its hiring practices, or it may fight in order to avoid giving other potential litigants the impression of being weak.

Cases where the potential settlement is small and the plaintiff has little chance of winning should be fought when there is a strong reason. Doing otherwise can lead to more and more nuisance suits.

Strategies for avoiding lawsuits are important for colleges and universities in today's legal environment. When faced with a legal challenge, the benefits of negotiation, direct attorney agreement, and arbitration should be considered.

The lower costs and faster process may be the best solution for everyone.

Public vs. Private Institutions

Higher education in this country has been strengthened by the development of quality public and private colleges and universities. When examining potential legal responsibilities and limitations, it is important to differentiate between the types of authority under which institutions of higher education operate.

The relationship of a private college to the law is generally established by a *charter*. The purposes of the institution and its method of governance are defined by this charter, and accompanying by-laws which provide operating principles. The charter may be issued by the state, and describe the laws under which private institutions are operated.

Constitutional guarantees — free speech, due process, equal protection, freedom of assembly, of the press, and from unreasonable searches and seizures — are not guaranteed on private college campuses. The language of the Constitution limits enforcement of these provisions to "state" action. Only where there is a showing of state action in private education will there be a finding of constitutional protections for individuals. What constitutes state action has been widely litigated in recent years. Most recently, the Civil Rights Restoration Act of 1988 has reestablished governmental controls in private institutions receiving governmental support, overturning the earlier limiting decision of *Grove City v. Bell* in the U.S. Supreme Court.

The status of public institutions is determined by the states. In establishing the college or university, institutional rights and responsibilities are enumerated or delegated. State laws control the extent to which public colleges operate "independently," and establish the nature of the legal relationships between the school and its students, and the school and its employees.

Because of the obvious "state" involvement in public higher education, full constitutional protections are extended to the campus setting.

In addition to grants of authority and constitutional concerns, legal relationships on campus can be of a *contractual* or *fiduciary* nature, for both private and public schools. The existence of an implied contract has been found in the language of college catalogs and the words of academic advisors. Where promises are made, through an application of contract laws, colleges and universities (or students) will be expected to perform. A fiduciary or "trust" relationship is established where a college is seen as knowing *what is needed* for education and knowing *in what environment* education should take place. Court deference to academic decisions is based on the fiduciary or trust concept.

In summary, the nature of an institution (public or private) can have great bearing on legal entanglements. The important legal distinctions between the authority of public and private colleges and universities needs to be understood before applying legal principles and developing legal responses.

1. Rights and Freedoms

There are those who may think it ironic that in our system of government the zealous protection of free speech requires that the mantle of free expression be extended to those who seek it so that they may advocate the violent overthrow of that very system, while condemning the right of others to express views opposed to their own. But the protection of the citizen in the expression and even advocacy of these views is vital in creating the vibrant atmosphere in which the search of scholarship can best flourish.
— *Franklin v. Atkins*, 409 F.Supp. at 445 (1976)

Ironic, indeed: The college campus is the place where the democratic ideal of "I may not agree with what you say, but will defend to the death your right to say it" may still ring true. Yet, allowing or even encouraging rabble-rousers can lead to disruption. The college or university has the difficult role of being guardian to the First Amendment, yet maintaining an orderly learning environment.

The late '60s and early '70s were a hot time for free speech cases springing from campuses. *Franklin* — originating in an incident at Stanford University in 1971 — was one of those. In the years since, the focus has shifted away from demonstrations and civil disobedience, although there are still such cases.

Below, we explore some other concerns under the broad heading of rights and freedoms: due process; religious freedom on campus; searches and seizures; AIDS; and speaker bans.

Due Process in Academe

In a line of cases, dating back to *Dixon v. Alabama State Board of Education*, 294 F.2d 150 (1961), courts have provided public colleges and universities with information on the requirements of the Constitution's due process clause in an effort to preserve "rudimentary elements of fair play." It was *Dixon* that first established the principles of notice and opportunity for hearing in campus disciplinary proceedings.

The most specific set of due process requirements established by the courts appears in *Esteban v. Central Missouri State College*, 277 F. Supp 649 (1967). After reviewing the college's suspension process, the court recommended the following rights and procedures:

- A written statement of the charges against an individual made available no less than 10 days before a hearing.

- A hearing before the person or persons having the power to expel or suspend.

- An opportunity to review evidence prior to the hearing.

- The right to have counsel at hearing, not necessarily to participate, but to advise an accused student.

- An opportunity to present one's own version of the facts and to present other evidence in support of the case.
- The right to hear evidence and ask questions of witnesses.
- A determination of the facts based only on the evidence as presented.
- A written statement of the findings.
- The right to make a record of the hearing at an individual's expense.

The *Esteban* requirements provide the most extensive judicial framework for use by college administrators in developing campus due process guidelines. Most courts, in reviewing campus procedures, have not insisted on full compliance with *Esteban*. Instead, in recognition of a need for some degree of administrative flexibility on campus, courts have generally required adherence to the principles, not the specifics, found in the *Esteban* decision.

Additional judicial guidance on due process notice and hearing requirements appears in *Jenkins v. Louisiana State Board of Education*, 506 F.2d 992 (1975), *Jones v. Tennessee State Board of Education*, 279 F.Supp. 190 (1968), and *Goss v. Lopez*, 419 U.S. 565 (1975).

These cases and others advise that charges should be written in sufficient detail to enable a student to present a defense at a hearing; that notice should be provided far enough in advance of a hearing to allow ample time to prepare a defense; that a hearing should precede suspension or expulsion unless a student's presence on campus poses a danger to persons, property, or the academic process; and that the formality of the disciplinary proceedings should increase with the severity of the potential penalties.

The right to an appeal process, a written record of the hearing, cross examination of witnesses, counsel, and use of formal rules of evidence are among the processes that may increase the fairness of a disciplinary hearing, but, while widely accepted, they have not been mandated by the courts as constitutional requirements.

"No one disputes the power of the university to protect itself by means of disciplinary action against disruptive students ... Pursuant to appropriate rule or regulation, the university has the power to maintain order by suspension or expulsion of disruptive students ... We do not require university codes of conduct to satisfy the same rigorous standards as criminal statues. We only hold that expulsion and prolonged suspension may not be imposed on students by a university simply on the basis of allegations of 'misconduct' without reference to any pre-existing rule which supplies an adequate guide." *Soglin v. Kauffman*, 418 F.2d 163 (1969).

The University and Religion

Does the use of university facilities by students, but for religious purposes, violate the establishment of religion clause in the Constitution? The First Amendment, as adopted in 1791, states: "Congress shall make no law respecting an establishment of religion, or prohibiting the free exercise thereof." Given the sensitive nature of religious organizational problems on campuses, college officials remain concerned by the implications of this question, often posed at law and higher education workshops. On the one hand government isn't supposed to support religion, and on the other, it isn't supposed to interfere with it. Where does letting students use campus facilities for worship fall?

The permissible use of university facilities by students for religious purposes was considered in *Keegan v. University of Delaware*, 349 A.2d 14 (1975). A group of students requested use of a public area in a university-owned residence hall for the purpose of holding worship services. The campus had a policy that prohibited such use, citing the establishment clause as support for the policy. The Delaware Supreme Court overturned a lower court decision and ruled in favor of the students' space request. In striking down the school policy, the court noted that no religious group would be given any special accommodation by a change in the policy (or that any special accommodation would be purely incidental). Granting the students' request was not found to be a violation of the establishment clause.

If *Keegan* seems relatively simple, the twists and turns in a later case show why administrators remain cautious about appearing to support the establishment of religion. In *Chess v. Widmar*, 480 F.Supp. 907 (1979), the University of Missouri had denied the use of its facilities for regular religious services. For support, the school cited an earlier case that had prohibited sectarian use of any college facility built under a federal higher education support program, *Tilton v. Richardson*, 403 U.S. 672. The court in *Chess* disagreed with the position taken in *Keegan* and ruled that regular use of a campus facility for religious services would violate the Constitution. However, on appeal, the decision in *Chess* was overturned. The appellate court (635 F.2d 1310) said that the university could not deny equal access to a public forum on the basis of the content of the message — religious, political, or any other. Thus, student organizations had a right to use school facilities for religious meetings.

The case was taken to the U.S. Supreme Court, where the appellate decision was upheld on free speech arguments. The court ruled: "In order to justify discriminatory exclusion from a public forum based on the religious content of a group's intended speech, the university must ... satisfy the standard of review appropriate to content-based exclusion. It must show that its regulation is necessary to serve a compelling state interest and that it is narrowly drawn to achieve that end."

It seems safe to conclude that public universities may allow students the use of facilities for religious purposes without violating the establishment clause of the Constitution. Denying the use of university facilities to religious student groups when they are made available to other campus organizations has been considered by the courts an unfair restriction on students' free expression rights under the First Amendment.

Who May Speak?

A dispute over students at Holy Cross College hiring Watergate conspirator G. Gordon Liddy for a lecture series renewed interest in a hot legal topic of the late 1960s and early '70s: speaker bans.

An associate dean at Holy Cross opposed the Cross and Scroll Society's payment of at least $5,000 to Liddy for a closed-door lecture on government. His objections sparked a loud campus debate on the issue of academic freedom.

The dean objected to any payment to Liddy, arguing that Liddy's notoriety derived solely from his status as a convicted felon, and that his credibility regarding how government runs was "weak at best." Liddy could come to campus and speak for free if he chose, but was not worth the money offered, the administrator asserted. (The sum offered represented nearly one-fourth of the student group's budget for the year; the group was one of the best-funded on campus.)

CLEAR AND PRESENT DANGER

In past years, colleges and universities have used a variety of methods in attempting to control or ban campus speakers. Most bans were struck down a decade ago on constitutional grounds as being prior restraints on free speech, or as being too vague or broad to enforce. The only remaining justification for banning speakers is to prevent a clear and present danger to a school and its programs. Under the First Amendment, the time, place, and manner of speech can be reasonably regulated, but speech may not be banned without evidence of campus danger.

Three cases have established the test for clear and present danger in campus speech conflicts. In *Molpus v. Fortune*, 311 F.Supp. 240, a federal court ruled that a university must prove, by clear and convincing evidence, that a speech will endanger the persons and property of the campus, or lead to the "forcible disruption or impairment of or interference" with the regular operations of the school.

In *Brooks v. Auburn University*, 412 F.2d 1171, a convicted felon was invited to speak. The school claimed his speech "might advocate breaking the law." The court ruled that more than mere fear of problems is necessary in order to deny speaking privileges, and quoted the Supreme Court case of *Brandenburg v. Ohio*, 395 U.S. 444: Speech is protected unless it is "directed to inciting or producing imminent lawless action and is likely to incite or produce such action."

Pickings v. Bruce, 430 F.2d 595, dealt with the definition of disruption of campus, one of the valid reasons for prohibiting speech. In that case, a student organization had invited a couple to campus to speak on biracial lifestyles. Fearing the speech would disrupt the campus, the school administration asked the student organization to cancel the program. The organization refused, their charter was suspended, the couple spoke anyway, and no disruption resulted. The court ruled that student organizations have a right to bring controversial speakers to campus. Concern that such speakers will provoke intense debate is not enough to justify intervention.

CLARITY COUNTS

Any regulations banning speakers, in addition to meeting the clear and present danger standard, must not be ambiguous or vague. They must be written so as to be clearly understood by all. Failure to clearly communicate restrictions can result in litigation, which may in turn lead to the striking down of campus speech rules as violations of the First and Fourteenth Amendments.

A 1968 case dealt with the vagueness issue. In *Dickson v. Sitterson*, 280 F.Supp. 486, the University of North Carolina invoked a state law designed to prohibit campus speech by persons involved in Communist-related activities or by advocates of the overthrow of the government. The federal court, reviewing a challenge to the law, ruled that the statute was so "vague that men of common intelligence must necessarily guess at its meaning and differ as to its application." The court struck down the statute as violating the due process clause of the Fourteenth Amendment.

Invitations to Dick Gregory and Dr. Timothy Leary to speak on campus were the subject of *Smith v. University of Tennessee*, 300 F.Supp 777. In that case, campus rules, not a state statute, limited the types of speakers allowed on campus. The rules included a ban on speakers defending themselves against accusations of crime, and a requirement that speakers be "competent." The court noted that prior restraints on speech "come to the courts with a heavy presumption against their constitutional validity." The guidelines were found to be too broad to be constitutional. Proper guidelines put limits on administrative discretion and prevent unrestricted censorship.

The Holy Cross dispute was resolved when the assistant dean decided not to block Liddy's campus appearance. He noted the issue had sparked more debate on campus than any other in the past decade.

Although the appearance got official approval, as a result of the Liddy incident a student-faculty group launched an investigation into how the campus lecture society makes decisions and handles money.

Can Students' Mail Be Seized?

Letters from home, packages containing cookies from Mom, and drugs — all arrive in the campus mail addressed to individual students. When it comes to the third item, what can administrators do? What are the limits of search and seizure here?

The arrest of two Tulane University students as they tried to claim a package containing $2,000 worth of powdered amphetamine from a local express mail office served as a reminder to administrators of the legal difficulties encountered in handling mail. The arrival of a suspicious-looking, or smelling, package on campus can have serious legal implications for all concerned.

A 1984 case, *Garman v. Forrest*, 741 F.2d 1069, dealt with the use of seized student mail as evidence in criminal proceedings. A package with a peculiar odor was delivered to a campus residence hall. Campus officials were alerted. They removed the package and brought in a dog trained to detect marijuana; the dog located the package while it was hidden in an office.

A public safety officer claimed the package and — under a local judge's supervision — opened it. It did contain marijuana. Officials then returned it to the dormitory for delivery to the student addressee. When the student claimed the package, police officers, armed with a search warrant, re-seized the package and arrested the student.

Criminal charges were eventually dismissed, but the student then sued the police, charging they had violated his First Amendment rights. No one had a right to intercept his personal mail and remove it for inspection, he claimed.

The court ruled, however, that officials can, in general, detain a package if there is reasonable cause to believe it contains an illegal substance. Delaying the mail may be justified if that allows time to obtain a valid search warrant in an ongoing investigation.

Colleges and universities with campus mail operations handling deliveries to or from students should take steps to insure that they are well-prepared to respond to the occasional suspicious package. A reasonable plan should include the following:

- Written campus policy establishing clear procedures for handling suspicious-looking packages and envelopes, including instructions concerning items that arrive already opened or damaged.
- Agreement in advance between campus officials and local law enforcement on how suspicious items are to be handled, stored, and (where appropriate) turned over to off-campus authorities.
- Effective training of staff in campus policies and procedures.
- Screening of staff involved in mail delivery to protect its integrity.
- Advance notice to students that suspicious-looking mail may be subject to detention and further investigation by campus or off-campus officers.

Charting the Route to a Good AIDS Policy

The American College Health Association (ACHA) has developed a set of recommendations for colleges and universities' responses to Acquired Immune Deficiency Syndrome (AIDS). Higher education administrators should seriously consider these recommendations as they develop and implement medically and legally sound campus policies. They should also review the legal implications of AIDS, and previously issued campus guidelines, in light of the new ACHA general statement.

The number-one response suggested by the ACHA is *education.* With no vaccine to prevent the illness, and no cure in sight, education becomes a responsibility for all those in a position to help halt its spread. Colleges and universities, because of their unique structure and relationships with students, have legitimate, substantial liability concerns about AIDS in their classrooms, residence halls, and workplaces. As in so many other liability matters, education is regarded as the best way to carry out the institution's responsibility to protect students, faculty, and staff. To quote the ACHA general statement, "as medical evidence consistently indicates that no actual safety risks are created in the usual workplace or academic setting, institutions can best render enrollment or employment safe and healthful through effective education and training programs."

ACHA recommends that all residence-hall staff, including students and employees, receive education about AIDS before new students arrive each term. Also, because of institutions' obligation to protect everyone to the fullest extent possible, AIDS education programs should use only up-to-date, reliable information. AIDS education materials should be "easily accessible and widely available."

SPECIFICALLY ...

The ACHA guidelines for institutional AIDS policies tackle many important areas of legal concern for campus administrators: admissions; use of facilities; residence halls; mandatory testing; confidentiality of information. Administrators should thoroughly review the liability issues the guidelines raise.

First, the courts would undoubtedly view the consideration of AIDS or HIV infection in any *admissions* process as unwarranted discrimination. Initial admissions decisions should not use infection as a criterion. In fact, it appears that persons with AIDS may legally have a *handicapping condition,* under Section 504 of the federal Rehabilitation Act. That statute decrees that "no otherwise qualified handicapped individual ... shall solely by reason of his handicap, be excluded from participation in, be denied benefits of, or be subjected to discrimination" under any program receiving federal assistance. In other words, those infected with the virus are entitled to equal protection of the law.

According to the best medical evidence available and the ACHA general statement, there is no justification for limiting *access to facilities* for those with or exposed to AIDS. This includes full use of campus gyms, pools, restaurants, student unions, theaters, and common areas. In addition, ACHA recommends that those infected be allowed to fully attend classes "as long as they are physically and mentally able."

Institutions' decisions about AIDS and *residential living* should be made on a case-by-case basis, according to the general statement. While ACHA notes there are no medical data indicating risks to those sharing a residence with an infected student, it advises caution in this area. Certainly, education in the residence halls is essential, to avoid unnecessary fear and anxiety; but assignment of single rooms to AIDS-infected persons may be necessary — for their own protection, not others'.

"AIDS and the College Campus," an earlier ACHA special report, sets out these guidelines for housing and residence life programs:

- form a group to respond to AIDS concerns
- identify individuals and units responsible for AIDS education
- train staff to identify on- and off-campus resources for AIDS counseling and testing
- train staff to understand liability concerning confidential information
- have staff encourage students to inform the health service of AIDS or related conditions, to insure quality medical care
- train staff to respond to parental concerns over AIDS in the residence halls
- do not allow concern or suspicion to lead to mandatory testing, relocation, isolation, or exclusion from campus housing.

AIDS IN THE INFORMATION AGE

Mandatory AIDS testing programs are "cost ineffective, counter-productive, and possibly discriminatory," to both students and staff, according to ACHA. Those who need to be tested for the HIV antibody should be referred to appropriate agencies by health services. That is not enough, however; education is needed to make sure those tested understand the *limitations* of current testing. Staff should be able to fully educate those who seek testing. And, campus facilities conducting testing must be fully aware of state laws and public health requirements on reporting and charting of results.

ACHA places strict requirements on facilities conducting AIDS testing, to insure the procedures are medically and legally sound. The general statement maintains that testing should only take place if it can be *confidential*; if the screening test results are confirmed by another procedure; and if pre-test and post-test counseling is required.

There are strong medical, legal, and ethical reasons for handling confidential information carefully. When one considers the sensitive implications for those with AIDS, care in handling that information becomes even more important. ACHA's advice that "no specific or detailed information concerning complaints or diagnosis be provided to faculty, administrators, or even parents, without the expressed written consent of the patient in each case" is consistent with standards for other confidential health information on campus.

The general statement questions whether infection data should even be included on ordinary medical records. The reason is the possibility of accidental release of individual AIDS patient information. If the fact of infection is to be recorded, the entry should be discussed in advance with the patient, both to protect the patient's rights, and to protect the institution from liability. Unauthorized release of medical information is the subject of state law as well as professional ethical standards, and only specific life-threatening situations justify violation of that confidentiality.

If confidential information is shared without authorization, legal liability for the institution can follow. Therefore, the ACHA guidelines conclude that "there is absolutely no medical nor other reason for institutions to advise students living in a residence hall of the presence there of students with HIV infection." Again, educational programming is the method of choice to create a safe residential or work environment.

One other section of the ACHA general statement deserves mention. It advises institutions to condemn any instances of *harassment*, including emotional or physical abuse, and respond swiftly to avoid further reactions.

Education and open communication remain the best approaches for dealing with the AIDS dilemma on campus. The virus by its nature raises complex issues, and our responses must be based on solid medical and legal advice. Colleges have a duty to protect members of the community from unreasonable risks; the ACHA general statement is designed to address the medical, social, legal, and ethical concerns administrators face in trying to perform that duty in the age of AIDS.

Principles

- Charges against a student should be written in sufficient detail to enable the student to present a defense at a hearing.

- Notice should be provided far enough in advance of a disciplinary hearing to allow ample time to prepare a defense.

- A hearing should precede suspension or expulsion unless a student's presence on campus poses a danger to persons, property, or the academic process.

- The formality of disciplinary proceedings should increase with the severity of the potential penalties.

- Public universities may allow students the use of facilities for religious purposes without violating the establishment clause of the Constitution.

- Denying the use of university facilities to religious student groups when they are made available to other campus organizations has been considered by the courts an unfair restriction on students' free expression rights under the First Amendment.

- Under the First Amendment, the time, place, and manner of speech can be reasonably regulated, but speech may not be banned without evidence of campus danger.

- Officials can, in general, detain a package if there is reasonable cause to believe it contains an illegal substance.

- Initial admissions decisions should not use AIDS infection as a criterion.

- No specific or detailed information concerning diagnosis of AIDS or complaints of AIDS-related symptoms should be provided to faculty, administrators, or even parents, without the expressed written consent of the patient in each case.

2. Security and Safety

Cornell University is a charitable institution.... We think a hospital's immunity from liability for the errors of surgeons and physicians is matched in the case of a university by a like immunity from liability for the errors of professors or instructors or other members of its staff of teachers.... The governing body of a university makes no attempt to control its professors and instructors as if they were its servants. By practice and tradition, the members of the faculty are masters, and not servants, in the conduct of the class room.... A university is not to answer in damages because ... a warning of the danger of some experiment has been inadvertently omitted, or because, either in performing the experiment or in supervising it, a teacher has combined the wrong ingredients or allowed them to be combined by others.

— *Hamburger v. Cornell University*, 148 N.E. at 541 (1925)

Universities are seldom referred to as charitable institutions these days. In fact, in light of the financial condition of some higher education institutions, some administrators may wish they were beneficiaries of charitable institutions.

Tort liability is a creature of state law, like many of the topics in this book. As such, it must always be presented with a disclaimer: "The laws of your state may vary." But most, if not all, states nowadays do hold higher education institutions liable in tort, whether they're charitable or not.

Besides tort liability, we look below at the issues of disruptive protests; vandalism; risk management; and fire prevention. You might be able to make some money along the way by hosting conferences or conventions on campus — safely.

Protest or Disruption?

How far can demonstrations go in the name of free speech? Mass gatherings and protests regularly prove the principle that colleges and universities are free marketplaces of ideas. Courts consistently maintain that students have a protected right to express views on campus through various means — including demonstrations. But the courts have set limits. Students may demonstrate as long as they do not (1) significantly disrupt campus operations, (2) interfere with the rights of others, or (3) destroy property. Much of the case law on campus demonstrations dates to the troubled 1960s; but the same principles are currently being applied — and tested — across the country.

The free speech provision of the First Amendment and the freedom of assembly and petition for redress of grievance clauses are the basis for most legal activity surrounding campus protests. The First Amendment to the Constitution states:

"Congress shall make no law respecting an establishment of religion or prohibiting the free exercise thereof; or abridging the freedom of speech, or of the press, or the right of the people peaceably to assemble, and to petition the Government for the redress of grievances."

While the wording of the First Amendment only restricts Congress, the Supreme Court extended the protections to acts of states as well. (*Schneider v. State*, 308 U.S. 147 (1939).) In addition, many state constitutions contain clauses that may apply First Amendment limitations to public and private institutions. (*State v. Schmid*, 423 A.2d 615 (1980), 70 L.Ed 2d 855 (1982).)

Tinker v. Des Moines School District, 393 U.S. 503 (1969), represents the standard legal reference. High school students had been suspended because they wore black armbands to class to protest U.S. involvement in Vietnam. In reviewing the case, the U.S. Supreme Court determined that such a protest was non-disruptive and students should not be punished for such acts. The Court noted that the First Amendment provides protection to "symbolic acts" done "for the purpose of expressing certain views." In sum, *Tinker* said, "First Amendment rights, applied in light of the special characteristics of the school environment, are available to teachers and students."

Healy v. James, 408 U.S. 169 (1972), brought *Tinker* to college campuses. There, a dispute over the recognition of a chapter of a local Students for a Democratic Society (SDS) organization at Central Connecticut State College made its way to the courts. *Healy* points out the important role the First Amendment has on college campuses. State colleges and universities are not immune from the sweep of the First Amendment. "The college classroom with its surrounding environs is peculiarly the 'marketplace of ideas,' and we break no new constitutional ground in reaffirming this nation's dedication to safeguarding academic freedom."

CLASSUS INTERRUPTUS

However, both *Tinker* and *Healy* make the point that freedom to protest is not permission to disrupt. In *Tinker*, "conduct by the student, in class or out of it, which for any reason — whether it stems from time, place, or type of behavior — materially disrupts classwork or involves substantial disorder or invasion of the rights of others is ... not immunized by the constitutional guarantee of freedom of speech." Colleges and universities can make rules to limit or prohibit protests that disrupt or seriously threaten to disrupt the educational process — for example, student protests that prevent campus personnel from using buildings by blocking the entrances.

Student protests which block building entrances have gone to court many times. In *Buttney v. Smiley*, 281 F.Supp. 280 (1968), the school suspended students for blocking entrances and failing to desist at university officials' request. Student arguments that university punishment violated their constitutional free speech rights got nowhere: The court ruled that the school legally punished them for what they did, not for what they were saying. In other words, the First Amendment and the Bill of Rights do not give students the right to block building access.

Campus "sit-ins" also have come under the scrutiny of judges and juries a number of times. Protesters at the University of Georgia arrived at the president's office to present a petition, were told he was out of town, and were arrested for not leaving after campus police asked them to. In *Alonso v. State*, 202 S.E.2d 37 (1973), the court ruled the use of criminal trespass charges against the students was constitutional. The First Amendment does not permit protesters to violate others' rights, and they did so by remaining in the office, disturbing others' work.

The *Alonso* court noted the students had met with a staff member, gotten a next-day appointment with the president, then been asked to leave. It concluded: "The rights protected by the First Amendment ... though fundamental, are not absolute, and must be tempered to a degree by the concepts of order and a healthy respect for the rights of other citizens."

Thus, when disruptive activity combines with First Amendment rights, courts have consistently sided with colleges' and universities' need to maintain educational operations free of disruption.

LIMITS ON THE LIMITS

Simple fear that something will happen to disrupt the educational process is not enough to support administrative action to limit freedom of expression. "Undifferentiated fear or apprehension of disturbance is not enough to overcome the right to freedom of expression" (*Tinker*). It is necessary for administrators to "reasonably forecast" that substantial disruption is imminent and base that forecast on actual evidence. It should also be noted that when the disturbance is or will be caused by spectators, not the protesters, university action should be taken against the onlookers, not the demonstrators.

Legal activity surrounding student protests over the 1980 situation in Iran also have helped clarify the limits colleges can place on student demonstrations. In *Shamloo v. Mississippi State Board of Trustees*, 620 F.2d 516 (1980), Iranian nationals supporting the government of Ayatollah Khomeini violated a Jackson State University regulation requiring three-day advance scheduling for protests, gatherings, and parades. A federal appellate court ruled that the protest was not disruptive or distracting and was a First Amendment protected activity. The court established two tests to determine if constitutional protections should be extended to specific protests. *Shamloo* concluded that the protest disruption must be "a material disruption of classwork," or that it must involve "substantial disorder or invasion" of the rights of others.

The reasonableness of university limitations on the time, place, and manner of protected speech was tested in *Bayless v. Martine*, 430 F.2d 872 (1970). In this case, students had been suspended for violating a university rule that limited demonstrations to a "student expression area" that could be reserved 48 hours in advance for non-violent purposes. Specific times for protest were established, but no restrictions were placed on the content of the demonstration. On review, the court noted that the advance notice requirement was a reasonable way of avoiding competing demonstrations, and allowed for time to arrange proper security.

Freedom of speech is not freedom to demonstrate anytime, anyplace. Cases such as *Buttney* and *Alonso* have upheld the principle that schools can take disciplinary action against protesters who disrupt campus operations, without violating the First Amendment. Administrators can legally maintain building and roadway access.

Perhaps the most concise legal guideline for dealing with campus demonstrations comes from *Esteban v. Central Missouri State College*, 415 F.2d 1077 (1969), where the court wrote:

"It is obvious that where there is actual or potentially disruptive conduct, or disorder, or disturbance ... or interference in the work of the school or of the rights of other students, or threats or acts of violence on the school premises ... then reasonable action by school authorities is constitutionally permitted. There must, however, be more than mere fear and apprehension of possible disturbance."

Avoid Liability in Your Summer Conference Business

In the unending search for dollars to support higher education, many see revenue from outside sources as the answer. One popular way to increase campus revenues using existing facilities is to create or expand a summer conference business.

A college campus presents an ideal setting for large or small summer meetings for many organizations. Campuses generally have plenty of residence hall, dining, meeting, and recreation space. Groups can thus plan meetings, seminars, conferences, or conventions between school terms. The idea is attractive to both parties. However, in addition to claims of unfair competition from local businesses, colleges and universities establishing or expanding summer conference businesses should know their legal duty to their guests — and be aware of risk-management steps that could eliminate or limit premises liability.

The status of an injured party in relation to the landowner generally determines the extent of premises liability. Three common-law classifications of status are possible: "trespasser," "licensee," and "invitee." Depending on the status, the law establishes a level of care the landowner must provide.

Common law establishes no duty to care for trespassers, such as those who climb fences and gates to enter. A landowner must protect a licensee from willful, wanton, or reckless conduct. The highest level of care, a duty to warn of hidden dangers, is reserved for invitees.

In many states, these common law classifications no longer determine landowner duty. Today, "the duty owed is one of reasonable care under the circumstances with foreseeability as the measure of liability" (*Eddy v. Syracuse University*, 78 A.D.2d 989 (1980)).

In the remaining common law states, the invitee classification is defined as follows: An invitee is on another's property for the other's benefit. A store customer, a theater patron, or a summer conference guest on campus exemplify invitees. Typically, the test is whether the landowner gets or expects a benefit from the invitee's presence. If there is a benefit or expectation, the visitor is an invitee and the landowner has a duty to exercise reasonable care to protect the guest. In the case of a summer conference guest, the institution has a duty to:

- not harm the guest through negligence;
- warn the guest of hidden hazards known to the institution;
- reasonably inspect the campus to discover possible hazards, both visible and hidden;
- protect guests from foreseeable dangers of using campus facilities; and
- render first aid or other care when the institution knows or should know that a guest is injured or ill.

To make sure the school is prepared to meet the necessary standard of care, administrators should: (1) develop a risk management plan to identify risks; (2) evaluate campus exposure to liability; and (3) help create a safe meeting environment. Conference planners must carefully inspect all campus facilities that will be used, and correct any problems that could lead to guest loss or injury.

Residence hall floors in use should have sprinklers for fire protection, and the location of the room and nearest emergency exit should be posted inside all room doors. Doors should have adequate locks, with chains if possible. Electrical cords should go behind furniture or along walls, and all lights should be working. All chairs should be in excellent condition. In bathrooms, tubs should have a rubber mat or non-slip surface, and shower heads should be secure to the wall.

Outside, campus walkways and parking lots should be well-lit and well-maintained. Swimming pools and fitness facilities should be well-staffed and maintained. Security personnel should be visible to guests, and visitors should know how to summon help if they need to.

When inspecting classrooms slated for meetings, include these items in your risk management evaluation: Rooms should be well-lit; aisles should be wide enough to accommodate expected crowds; exit signs should be in appropriate locations. (Obviously, exits should never be obstructed in any way.) Tables and chairs in meeting rooms should be in excellent condition; audio-visual equipment should be in good working order. Floor cables should be taped down.

Some other general considerations to review: Registration or check-in tables should be in a prominent location, and the area should be well-lit; all carpeting should be in good condition; all guests should have emergency telephone numbers. Elevators should be in good operating condition, and stop level with floors, not above or below, to prevent slip-and-fall accidents.

In addition, meeting planners should know the name of a local physician, and have the location of the nearest hospital on hand.

Campuses can be excellent hosts for summer conferences. However, to insure that both host and guests have adequate protection, sound risk management strategies are needed — before, during, and after the summer months.

Slipping, Tripping, and Falling on Campus

A slip-and-fall on a discarded banana peel may be the oldest Vaudeville gag in the world, but it's an example of what remains a very active area of college and university law. Every day thousands of students, staff, and guests walk across campuses safely. But a few slip and fall, and these incidents often result in legal action. The basic claim is negligence — that the school, as landowner, did not properly maintain its premises or failed to warn of danger.

Potential slip-and-fall sites are everywhere on campus. Sidewalks, staircases, parking lots, residence halls, rest rooms, and construction sites have all been starting points for campus litigation. A look at some examples suggests that prevention is the best medicine:

A Minnesota student, crossing campus on foot during the second day of a three-day blizzard, slipped and fell on an icy sidewalk. Her negligence suit against the school netted a $42,000 damage award, even though the condition of the sidewalk had been obvious to all. The court said the school had an obligation to safely maintain its property at all times. The college appealed, saying the extraordinary weather made maintenance temporarily impossible.

The appeals court agreed with the school, ruling that a reasonable amount of time must be allowed for maintenance under unusual weather conditions. The college had tried, but failed to keep the walks clear during the storm. While agreeing with the lower court that a landlord or property owner must maintain its property in a safe condition, the court dismissed the action because of the extreme conditions present in this case. *Nieman v. Northwestern*, 389 N.W.2d 260 (1986).

HIDDEN PERIL

The *Nieman* case has limited application, however: The same argument, applied to a different case with different facts, was unsuccessful. In *Isaacson v. Husson College*, 332 A.2d 757 (1975), the campus roads had been cleared after a storm, but not the sidewalks. The court found that a reasonable physical plant director would have known that ice would form on the sidewalks and then be covered by blowing snow, creating a hidden danger. Reasonable time had passed to allow clearing of the sidewalk before a student fell on it. The court awarded damages of $12,000 to the injured student.

Another school, also claiming inadequate time to make an area safe, lost the argument and $10,000 in damages to a student who fell on campus. School had remained open during a storm, and maintenance crews were working on clearing icy spots when the accident happened. The court held: "The large size of the defendant's property does not absolve it from its duty" to maintain a reasonably safe campus. The court noted that the campus had notice of the danger, and failed to correct it soon enough. *Shannon v. Washington University*, 575 S.W.2d 235 (1978).

These cases do not provide an exact measure of how much time is enough to clear ice and snow. But certain guidelines emerge: First, the decision to keep a campus open during a storm should be made with care. Second, if the campus does remain open, "reasonable" clearing means keeping drives and sidewalks clear, and getting them clear as soon as possible. It takes a heck of a storm (such as a three-day blizzard) for the courts to allow maintenance crews much lag time. Third, the size of the campus appears to make no difference in what is "reasonable."

FAIR WARNING

A case not involving ice and snow provides more insight into "reasonableness." A student, not seeing a newly-dug construction excavation, fell into it and was burned by steam pipes and hot water. She sued, charging the college had failed to warn her of the danger and failed to maintain the area safely. The court agreed, noting that since the school had dug the hole, it could not argue that it did not have notice of the danger to pedestrians. That knowledge should have been shared with those likely to come in contact with the danger. The school must provide due warning of dangers that are known or should be known. *Prairie View A&M University v. Thomas*, 684 S.W.2d 169 (1984).

As the *Prairie View* case illustrates, what school officials might consider "obvious," courts might consider "notice" to the school that a warning or repair is needed.

And finally, a college slip-and-fall banana case (although there is no peel involved). A student leaving classes noticed the floor was slippery, took a few steps, then fell, injuring her back. The night before, a custodian had improperly applied banana oil on the hardwood floors, creating a hazard. While there was no posted notice of the danger, the student was aware of the floor's condition. Despite her knowledge, the court ruled that it was not unreasonable for her to venture onto the floor to test it. The college's claim that she should have avoided the danger known to her was unsuccessful, and the court awarded damages. *Lumbard v. Fireman's Fund Insurance Company*, 302 So.2d 394 (1974).

Taking the case law in this area as a whole, school officials should consider the following principles and facts, keeping in mind that students are "invitees":

- An owner must warn an invitee of obstructions on a path.
- A school has a duty to maintain premises which includes inspecting and discovering dangerous conditions.
- The owner of property is assumed to be aware of a danger if a reasonably prudent person would have or should have known of it.
- Awards beyond actual expenses are not uncommon. In *Isaacson*, the student's medical costs were $1,600; the court awarded $12,000.
- Finally, when a school is open for business, there is an implied warranty of safety for all. If an area of the campus is not safe, for whatever reason, campus visitors are entitled to warning. *Rawlings v. Angelo State University*, 648 S.W.2d 430 (1983).

Failure to warn is negligence.

Better Management of Risks
Means a Better Campus

Risk management, practiced in the private sector for many years, has now come to college and university campuses. Exposure to losses through liability is part of any activity or operation, on or off campus. We have looked in detail at several areas of tort risk in higher education. Having explored the potential for loss — injury, death, and financial damages — we can readily see the need for a campus process to handle liability exposure through risk management programming.

Risk management *protects a school's resources* by reducing the potential for loss. An effective program of risk management (as developed in the private sector) has four basic components:

- Risk Identification
- Risk Evaluation
- Risk Treatment
- Program Implementation

Through a concentrated risk management effort, an institution can avoid devastating personal *and* institutional financial losses.

LOOKING AROUND

The first phase of risk management, risk *identification*, is the process of determining *where* on campus there is potential for tort liability. There are four general categories of exposure: tort, contractual, property, and fidelity. *Tort* liability involves personal injury; *contractual* exposure relates to disputes over agreements; *property* damages may be caused by natural disasters and other factors; *fidelity* risks are generally associated with handling of funds and products.

A variety of means is available to handle identification of campus risks. Private institutions with insurance coverage can utilize the services of insurance carriers to help them review areas of potential loss. Outside consulting firms are also available in most areas to conduct reviews of exposure. Don't forget the existing institutional staff; they can effectively identify potential problems because they're familiar with the campus, its operations, facilities, and procedures. Staff members can develop their own assessment process, or modify existing analysis programs.

Through whatever means, identification of the potential for loss is crucial to successful risk management. Once you identify what the problem areas are, you can then categorize them as tort, contract, property, and fidelity problems for purposes of risk *evaluation*.

LOOKING AHEAD

Risk evaluation for college campuses is the process of determining the *probability* of loss, the predictability of loss during a given period, the maximum and minimum level of projected loss, and the campus resources available to cover losses. By analyzing already identified risks this way, and determining the likelihood and potential dollar level of losses, you can best determine the need for action. For example, if you determine that only a few accidents of small financial consequence are likely in one area (such as the new ceramics studio), you should take a different approach there than in areas of high risk with great potential dollar losses — such as your new program to have armed National Guardsmen on retainer to put down campus unrest.

Through risk identification and evaluation, you can both review areas of possible loss and understand the likelihood and consequences of those losses. Armed with that knowledge, you are in a position to decide how to best protect the institution.

TAKING THE TREATMENT

Risk *treatment* approaches available to colleges and universities include:

- Risk avoidance
- Risk reduction
- Risk retention, and
- Risk transference.

Selection of a specific risk treatment depends on the likelihood of loss and the possible size of the loss.

Risk *avoidance* involves complete elimination of the hazard — cancellation of field trips, banning fraternities and sororities, or removing trampolines and diving boards from recreation facilities, for example. In making this decision, a school must always weigh the potential benefit of a program or activity against the potential for loss. Of course, complete elimination of risks is impossible in today's higher education environment. But where the exposure to risk greatly outweighs any possible benefit to the campus community, you should consider risk avoidance.

Risk *reduction* involves acting to lower the likelihood of injury or loss, or to reduce the level of losses should they occur. Even when a school has insurance coverage, it remains important to reduce the potential for loss. The savings from fewer and less severe injuries and losses obviously is measured in more than dollars. You must take all possible steps to insure the safety of people and property on campus.

Risk reduction in the area of tort liability centers on four basic steps:

- development of safety rules for people, equipment, and facilities;
- periodic safety inspections;
- effective preventive maintenance for campus equipment, facilities, and property; and
- adequate training for employees in safety, emergency procedures, and first aid.

These measures are designed to lower the frequency and severity of campus accidents, and reduce the dollar loss of damages when accidents do happen.

Colleges assume a certain level of risk by simply opening their doors in the morning. *Retention* of risks is really a form of self-insurance, in which administrators decide to continue an operation or activity despite its risks. In choosing to retain a risk, ask these questions:

1) Is there no way to transfer the risk, or eliminate the potential for loss?

2) Is the maximum possible loss small enough that the school's resources can cover it?

3) Is the likelihood of loss so low that the potential can be ignored?

4) Would it, or could it, cost as much to transfer the risk as it could cost to pay the damages from loss?

Shifting the potential for loss to another party or agency is the fourth risk-treatment method available to administrators. Risk *transfer*, when properly used, provides protection against financial loss. You should transfer risks when a program must continue, but the institution cannot absorb the potential loss.

Risk transfers are possible through a variety of means. Purchase of insurance is the most basic method. For a price, an insurance carrier commits to bearing the consequences of all or specific campus programs and activities. Other common means of transferring risks: subcontracting for services; requiring liability waivers; hold-harmless clauses in contracts; leasing facilities; and requiring users of campus facilities to carry liability insurance which names the institution as an additional insured.

Risk treatment methods — avoidance, reduction, retention, and transfer — are available options *after* you have fully identified and evaluated campus risks. Which specific methods you use is entirely dependent on the likelihood and extent of losses.

The final element of a good campus risk management program is *implementation*, putting into effect all that's been learned from previous steps. An informed, trained, and committed staff is critical here.

An institutional commitment to risk management, through proper risk identification and evaluation, selection of treatment, and program implementation, is a must for the safety of the campus community — and for the financial stability of the institution itself.

Manage risks; don't let losses manage you!

Residence Hall Fires
Should Spark Preventive Action

A number of frightening stories about college residence hall fires appeared in the news not long ago:

- In Delaware, two Wesley College students were charged with igniting a dormitory fire with a smoke bomb, apparently meant as a prank. One student died and four were injured, one seriously. Police charged the two with manslaughter and criminal mischief. After the fire, students complained that the dormitory fire alarm did not function properly.

- Scores of students were evacuated from a residence hall at Lawrence University (Wisconsin) when a burning candle started a fire that caused $60,000 damage and slightly injured four students. One student said that he entered a room in the hall and saw a small fire in the corner. It swiftly spread to wall tapestries and bedding. Smoke soon filled the 144-bed building, forcing emergency evacuation.

- At Eastern Michigan University, there were 10 reported residence hall fires in a single month. All occurred in a multiple dormitory/conference center complex. After an earlier fire that resulted in six injuries and $120,000 damage, officials had placed 24-hour-a-day security patrols in the complex.

The fires that happen on campus are not unusual. But because of the *concentration of students in relatively small living areas*, fires here present a *greater danger to life*. History shows that campus fires are most likely to start in dormitory rooms, and this fact puts a high level of responsibility and liability on administrators' shoulders.

Identification of hazards is the key to preventing fires on campus. School personnel must *regularly inspect* campus buildings with an eye toward the fire potential in all areas. Many campus fire hazards are obvious, such as:

- inadequate room or building exits
- portable heaters
- combustible interior finishes, which can give off unusual smoke or toxic gases

- open flames or burners
- overloaded or poorly placed electrical outlets.

Room decorations can create dangerous fire conditions if not controlled. Flammable holiday decorations led to a 1977 dormitory fire at Providence College (Rhode Island) that killed 10 students. Three Philadelphia fraternity members died in a 1967 fire involving party decorations.

Common student decorating practices are hazardous. For example, students often attach paper posters to walls, doors, windows, and ceilings. (Watch for flammable items in the path of room or building exits.) They also put carpeting on walls or hang parachutes, blankets, cloth wall hangings, or nets from ceilings.

Common sense is the best guide to preventing accidental fires. But what about when it's no accident?

Arson presents a lurking danger in any group living environment. *Visible security* can prevent firesetting in residence halls. Campus officials should *inspect dormitories regularly* for conditions that encourage or discourage disturbed persons determined to set fires. For example, fire officials warn that leaving scorched areas visible after small fires often invites follow-up fires. They advise covering or painting over scorched walls, doors, or bulletin boards as soon as possible.

Two considerations are paramount in evaluating overall campus fire danger and developing a fire safety plan.

Design factors of campus buildings, such as number and types of exits, types of windows, location of heating and storage materials, and general susceptibility to spread of fire, are critical. Also in this category are fire alarm systems, extinguishers, and smoke detectors.

Training and education of students and staff are important to any effort to reduce liability for fire. In academic settings where there is potential for fire, such as laboratories, instructors should teach students fire safety. In residence halls, staff should provide residents materials on fire safety and emergency exits. It's smart to make all faculty and staff aware of the liability the institution faces if they fail to educate their students on the dangers of and responses to fire.

No matter what the circumstances are, the public, students, and parents will *hold the college liable for basic safety* of students on campus. The fires at Wesley, Lawrence, and Eastern Michigan should serve as reminders to college officials of the *continuing need for prevention.* If any reinforcement of this point is necessary, the pain and suffering of victims, large monetary losses from multi-million-dollar lawsuits, and escalating insurance premiums should be enough.

Vandalism: Ways of Tackling It

The causes of vandalism on college campuses are, by all accounts, complex and varied. But with both the incidence and the cost of campus vandalism on the rise, schools must understand the causes, establish goals in attacking the problem, and develop strategies for preventing acts of destruction.

In a classic study ("The Politics of Vandalism," *New Society*, Dec. 1968, pp. 872-78), sociologist Stanley Cohen breaks vandalism down into six categories:

Acquisitive Vandalism. Carried out in order to steal either money or property; frequent on college campuses. Breaking into a vending machine is an example.

Tactical Vandalism. Designed to achieve a desired end; a conscious act with a goal. Destruction of fire-alarm bells, to prevent them from ringing in the halls and disturbing students, is an example.

Ideological Vandalism. Acts of revenge or retribution by an angry student; often directed at residence-hall staff.

Play Vandalism. Done in the context of games or competition. Contests to break the most ceiling tiles or fire extinguisher boxes without being seen fall into this category.

Malicious Vandalism. The most violent type of destructive behavior; a direct expression of rage or frustration.

Most studies of vandalism have concentrated on the inner city, not the college campus. However, the limited data available reveal several trends concerning *who* campus vandals are:

- Men are involved far more frequently than women.
- Drinking is very common prior to acts of destruction.
- Freshmen are more involved in destructive activities than others.
- Most vandals live on campus and vandalize their own residence halls.
- Stress, resulting from personal relationships, is often a factor.
- Vandalism is usually a spontaneous act arising from group interaction or particular situations.

In an effort to better understand vandalism's roots, the Association of College and University Housing Officers (ACUHO) conducted an on-campus study in 1981. Their research found seven primary causes of dormitory damage: alcohol abuse; attitude of residents to group living, design, condition, and age of the residence halls; anxiety and stress; lack of activities; reaction to discipline; damage by non-residents; and crowded conditions. Far and away, campuses named *alcohol* as the leading factor in intentional campus damage.

Whatever the cause of damage due to vandalism, institutions must respond aggressively to reduce the losses of time, resources, and morale that go with it. A 1985 University of Maryland study on "Group Billing and Security Deposits" established two universal goals for reducing problems of vandalism: general *shaping* of student behavior coupled with *addressing specific* damage problems.

Goals of shaping behavior are:
- create a residence-hall environment which is self-disciplined;
- have an atmosphere in the halls conducive to sleep, study, and socializing;
- provide a safe, secure living environment;
- have an environment which, through policies, programs, and procedures, complements the students' classroom experience;
- provide housing services which are satisfying to residents; and
- have an environment in which students show respect for each other and for the facility.

In addressing damage and vandalism specifically, the Maryland study identified the following goals, which are applicable to most campuses:
- protect and preserve the quality of the residence halls;
- maintain and improve the dorms;
- improve student respect for the facilities;

- improve employee morale;
- reduce the number of damage incidents;
- have individuals and groups take responsibility for damage;
- punish those involved through judicial systems or billings;
- deter residents from acts of vandalism;
- recover costs associated with intentional vandalism; and
- increase student involvement in anti-damage programs.

Establishing the goals for a campus program is only the second step in a campus anti-vandalism campaign's development and implementation. That step must be followed by creation of action strategies to address the causes of vandalism. A 1983 study at the University of Connecticut developed a variety of campus activities designed to contain the problem.

An important part of any vandalism reduction program is *publicity* to attract support for the program. Publicity efforts generally should start at the beginning of the school year, and be regularly reinforced during the year. Among the recommended publicity strategies:

- student-designed anti-vandalism posters
- articles in campus and local newspapers
- hats and buttons with damage-control theme
- campus radio public-service spots or newspaper ads featuring campus sports figures
- a Vandalism Prevention Week
- discussion groups with student government and residence-hall staff
- recognition for environment-improvement programs in the halls.

Together with publicity campaigns, *primary* strategies to improve the environment are necessary. Some examples:

- residence hall space-personalizing contests
- environmental wellness programs for students and staff
- study of student use of dormitory space
- designing and painting common areas
- encouraging faculty to conduct vandalism-related research
- improving relations with campus police
- encouraging classroom assignments pertaining to vandalism issues
- support for campus special-interest housing.

Deterrent strategies aim to raise the risk of vandals' behavior. They include:
- surveys of other schools to assess systems/methods used to measure campus vandalism
- study of occurrences of vandalism by sex, date, time, location, and type
- review of student perceptions of vandalism; examination of campus judicial responses
- initiation of a system of direct billing for vandalism charges.

Technical strategies attempt to develop an area of compromise between a vandal-proof and flexible environment, one which responds to both students' and administrators' needs. A summary of technical strategies:

- annual inspections, and examination of trends in vandalized areas, to determine what areas are susceptible
- purchase of vandal-resistant furnishings for dormitories
- inclusion of vandalism concerns in rehabilitation and improvement projects
- provision of appropriate security measures and hardware in residence halls.

A final stage of any vandalism-prevention effort should be an *examination of program effectiveness*. The data collected should help campuses refine programs and achieve established goals. Through solid understanding of vandalism's causes, establishment of attainable student-behavior and damage-control goals, implementation of strategies to address the problem, and evaluation of the effort, campuses can aggressively pursue the elimination, or at least the limitation, of damage due to vandalism.

Principles

- Colleges and universities can make rules to limit or prohibit protests that disrupt or seriously threaten to disrupt the educational process.
- Schools can take disciplinary action against protesters who disrupt campus operations, without violating the First Amendment.
- An institution has a duty to reasonably inspect the campus to discover possible hazards, both visible and hidden, and protect guests from foreseeable dangers.
- Reasonable clearing means keeping drives and sidewalks clear, and getting them clear as soon as possible after a storm.
- If an area of the campus is not safe, for whatever reason, campus visitors are entitled to warning.
- Risk treatment methods — avoidance, reduction, retention, and transfer — are available options *after* you have fully identified and evaluated campus risks.
- Training and education of students and staff are important to any effort to reduce liability for fire.
- Schools must understand the causes of vandalism, establish goals in attacking the problem, and develop strategies for preventing acts of destruction.

3. Student Services

For many years it has been the practice of the governing authorities of Berea College to distribute among the students at the beginning of each scholastic year a pamphlet entitled "Students Manual," containing the rules and regulations of the college for the government of the student body. Subsection 3 of this manual, under the heading "Forbidden Places," enjoined the students from entering any "place of ill repute, liquor saloons, gambling houses," etc. During the 1911 summer vacation, the faculty, pursuant to their usual practice of revising the rules, added another clause to this rule as to forbidden places ... "(b) Eating houses and places of amusement in Berea, not controlled by the college, must not be entered by students on pain of immediate dismission...."

  — *Gott v. Berea College,* 161 S.W. at 205 (1913)

Businessmen these days are actively pursuing claims against colleges and universities for unfair business competition, but in 1913 colleges didn't have to put up with any of that. They *eliminated* the competition.

As the student service arena has gotten more complicated, it has also gotten more dangerous. There is the possibility of dram shop liability; the hassle of controlling damage to dormitories without imposing martial law; and the complications afforded by the growing incorporation of student services, as well as unfair business competition:

Residence Hall Group Billing and Security Deposits

Was it wear and tear? An accident? Perhaps negligence? Or was it vandalism? Those are the questions faced daily by administrators and students in college and university residence halls when damage is discovered. Two of the most common approaches in paying for repairs, when no one can be identified as being responsible, are student group billing and security deposits.

Group billing involves assessing damages that can't be identified as being caused by any specific individual or group of individuals and charging them to all residents in a particular residence hall unit. They are all billed in equal shares for the cost of repairing damage to public or common areas in residence halls.

Security deposits require an advance payment by residents to cover the cost of necessary repairs related to damage during the course of the year. These systems can have provisions to charge the accounts of those responsible or group-bill everyone living in the area.

DOUBLE BIND

During the past two decades, courts have become more willing to place civil rights-based limitations on student conduct rules and regulations at colleges and universities. The amount and dollar value of dormitory damage has dramatically increased during the same period, and institutions of higher education have been faced with the dual challenge of reducing vandalism and repairing residence halls with limited resources.

Group billing is generally used when damage has been done to a common or "public" area in residence halls and no individual or group of individuals can be identified as being responsible. Many group billing systems have a feature that allows for a grace period to encourage the involved parties to come forward on their own or be identified by others. When this fails, the cost of damage repairs is assessed against everyone living in the area. This leads to a situation where individuals not responsible for damage, directly or indirectly, are forced to pay for its repair.

The most commonly identified problem with group billing is uncertainty over whether it's legal. Under these systems, innocent parties are knowingly treated as if they are guilty. A basic tenet of our system of laws, the presumption of innocence, is seemingly violated by group billing, although few legal cases exist to provide any clear sense of direction to colleges and college residence-hall students on the matter.

It appears that many legal tests of the principle have been settled out of court, leading to the resolution of specific problems, but not providing much guidance to others with similar concerns. The relatively large number of out-of-court settlements is due in part to the generally small sums involved in most group billing disputes. A thousand dollars in attorney's fees and court costs to challenge a $300 group damage charge may seem to be smart politics, but it's a poor choice economically for most students.

A New York case, *Lefkowitz v. Bel Fior Hotel*, 408 N.Y.S. 696 (1978), deals in part with the central issue in university-student group billing disputes. A hotel that rented rooms to community college students had a clause in its rental agreement that allowed for the costs of damage to be deducted from security deposits. In the event that no one could be identified as having direct responsibility for damage, the reasonable cost of repair could be deducted from all the security deposits on an allocated basis. The state disagreed and took the matter to court.

A lower court sided with the state and the students on the key problem with group billing. "Each student is required to pay for damages in the event the respondent (hotel) cannot determine to whom the damage is attributable. This is inherently unfair on its face since an innocent student would then be paying for damage caused by another student." (*Lefkowitz* at 699.)

However, the state appellate division reversed the decision, saying a contract's a contract and the students agreed to the terms, including the group billing provision. In striking down the lower court decision against group billing, the appellate court did not support the argument that the contract was unfair on its face. It simply established a contractual standard that must be reviewed and adhered to in similar agreements.

In another case, an American Civil Liberties Union challenge to a Rutgers University group billing process dealt with three related concerns: the definition of the procedure; the need to communicate the policy to residence-hall students; and the need for an established appeal process.

The court required the university to more clearly define the need and purpose of the process, to develop a more effective means of communicating the process to students, and to establish an appeals procedure to insure compliance with due process requirements.

(For additional materials on this case and related cases, see "Group Billing in College Residence Halls: Is It Defensible?", 88 Dick. L.Rev. 497 (1984), by Carolyn Angelo.)

NOT ENOUGH SECURITY

The 1985 University of Maryland study on security deposits which we referred to in Chapter 2 in connection with vandalism concluded that the "use of security deposits in themselves will not eliminate the unassigned damage problem." Only one of 29 schools responding to the survey indicated that a security deposit alone led to any decrease in damage due to vandalism. There is a general feeling that a system of advance security deposits, without a group billing procedure, does not provide students with the proper opportunity or attitude to improve conditions. Some may simply damage up to their "limit." A security deposit may collect repair dollars up front, but does little to control vandalism.

Almost 70% of the schools responding to the survey had a group billing system and a third of the colleges had security deposits.

(For more materials on security deposits and group billing, consult "Group Billing and Security Deposits as Responses to the Problem of Damage and Vandalism in Residence Halls at the University of Maryland at College Park," 1985, by Thomas A. Scheuermann and Peter K. Sullivan, available from the University of Maryland Residence Life Dept., 3117 N. Administration Bldg., College Park, MD 20742. Cost: $6.50.)

Group billing and security deposits have become standard methods of dormitory damage control. However, the legal foundations for these efforts have not been fully explored. The individual rights of residence hall students need to be maintained, and no matter what policy is used, steps should be taken to insure that there is a need for the process, that the purpose of the program is clearly defined, that the policy is effectively communicated to residence-hall students, and that an appeal process exists. All systems should resort to group billing only after every effort has been made to identify the individuals actually responsible for damage, and the use of a security deposit-only system should be carefully reviewed to make sure that the system will achieve the results expected. The "presumption of innocence," even in cases of residence-hall damage due to vandalism, should be maintained to the greatest degree possible.

Don't Hesitate — Incorporate!

During the past two decades legally sanctioned student corporations — service, professional, and educational — have bloomed on college campuses nationwide. Student corporations now provide bookstores, food stores, residence halls, travel agencies, and even health-care services, greatly extending students' role in managing student life outside the classroom. As the trend continues, administrators should better understand the principles behind not-for-profit student corporations. On the other hand, students who are both managers and consumers of services should better understand the responsibility and liability that officers and directors of corporations have.

Students aren't the only ones on campus involved in corporations. Faculty and staff are often asked to serve on boards of directors of campus corporations such as bookstores, food services, child-care centers, as well as professional organizations. They, too, should understand their rights and responsibilities when acting as a board member or officer.

Faculty-staff interest and developmental organizations have also become more active, and more organized, in recent years. Every such national organization has state or regional affiliates, and all can have boards of directors. Campus personnel often act as directors of these not-for-profits.

MEETING THE NEED

In the early 1970s, student corporations developed to give students services they generally couldn't get on campus. At the same time, these corporations established independence from campus administration. The fact that incorporation affords a degree of protection from personal liability (see below) certainly did nothing to hurt the trend. But in many cases, schools themselves encouraged development of on-campus student corporations. They saw that students could provide services for themselves beyond anything the administration could do. On top of that, it meant that students would have direct control of and responsibility for difficult activities, such as student newspapers. As students wanted more services, at lower cost, and wanted services for different beliefs and lifestyles that schools could not easily support, they discovered that the not-for-profit corporation is the proper vehicle to provide them.

The traditional problem of student leadership turnover meets its solution in the corporate management structure, a continuing entity dictated by law. This structure, with its board of directors and officers elected from the board, provides greater leadership opportunities to more students. Through board involvement, it also allows for development of future leadership, and requires decision-making through a democratic, consensus-building process. Because of these factors, many see the student service corporations as a way to separate student politics from student services.

Campus-based professional service and professional development organizations have also incorporated in recent times, but for far different reasons. Legal not-for-profit status helps professional-interest organizations get donations, since donors enjoy tax benefits in return for their generosity. In addition, the insurance and liability crisis of the last few years has served as a reminder of the need for *protection from liability*. Corporation law provides personal-asset protection to its managers and members by making the corporation — a separate "person" under the law — responsible for liabilities and obligations. Fear of personal liability has driven many previously unincorporated campus professional service or development organizations to seek more protected status for their members.

GROUND RULES

State laws control non-profit corporations, and state laws always differ. However, there are some basic principles that apply to campus service and professional corporations that everyone working with them or for them should understand.

The basic management structure, regardless of the corporation's size or purpose, is a board of directors responsible for its workings. Responsibilities can be delegated (to committees or employees), but the *ultimate authority, and responsibility, remains with the board of directors*, whether faculty, students, staff, or a combination.

Directors and officers of corporations must carry out their duties in "good faith," with the same care that any prudent person would exercise in similar circumstances. The good-faith standard suggests that you will not be held liable for an *incorrect* decision, as long as the decision was *reasonably* made. This means that not-for-profit directors must carefully consider options; seek outside help when needed; and make decisions only after open, frank discussion. Carrying out corporate duties really amounts to using common sense, plus informed judgment, in making decisions.

To whom are these campus corporations accountable? First, to the not-for-profit corporation itself. The directors' and officers' job is to protect and advance the organization's interests. Second, to the corporation's membership: the student body, the campus community, or those involved in the organization. An officer or director has a duty to serve their needs, a duty established by the corporation's governing documents (certificate of incorporation and by-laws). Finally, in many states, a campus service or professional corporation has an ultimate responsibility to the public, and to the state, when its services or goals extend into the community.

Be aware of two legal principles that may affect those involved in non-profits:

- A member of a board with special knowledge, from previous training, education, or experience, will be held to a higher standard of care, based on that knowledge.
- The law has general prohibitions against self-dealing; so directors and officers must always be on the lookout for conflicts of interest.

Serving as an officer or director of a student service or professional-development corporation is an honor, but one which carries with it great responsibilities. If you don't have the necessary time or interest, don't accept the position. Remember, *board members can be held responsible for all actions of the board, even if they don't attend every meeting where those actions are taken.* Therefore, board members should regularly attend meetings, and carefully review all relevant documents — by-laws, committee reports, and financial statements.

WHO'S LIABLE?

A key reason for incorporation: the protection of the membership from *personal liability* for the corporation's debts and obligations. Members need not fear losing personal assets because of corporate activities if things go wrong. However, many states' laws do allow for directors' personal liability when there is "waste" of assets by directors; unpaid employee wages; or failure to properly carry out donors' instructions.

A director or officer who is sued for breach of duty often has some protection from the corporation in the form of *indemnification* for expenses involved in defending the lawsuit. The corporation or professional organization spells out in its by-laws under what circumstances it will cover expenses (e.g., not in cases of negligence), and which expenses ("reasonable" ones, including attorneys' fees). In other words, where the sued officer reasonably believed her actions were in the organization's best interests, that organization covers her costs in defending or appealing the suit.

Aside from indemnification clauses, many states in recent years have passed laws further protecting non-profits' officers and directors. Most of these statutes apply to agencies operated "exclusively for religious, charitable, scientific, literary, or educational purposes." (The language is from Internal Revenue Service Code section 501(c).) The purpose is to encourage unpaid directors and officers to keep on doing what they're doing by removing the threat of personal liability — except in cases of gross negligence or malice.

Various needs have driven the rise in non-profit campus operations, and in turn, those new operations have met those needs — more and cheaper student services, protection of members from personal liability, and so on. But it is important that persons involved in campus corporations remember both the rights and responsibilities. *Corporations are accountable* — to the directors, to the membership, to the campus, to the community.

Control Campus Liquor Sales

Even though changes in states' legal minimum drinking ages have radically altered the population of drinkers on campus, many colleges and universities continue to sell alcoholic beverages. With suits over liquor liability almost as plentiful as alcohol itself, every college needs to stop and take stock of its liquor policies to protect itself from avoidable suits.

All states control the sale of alcohol; most require vendors to have a license. In addition, most states have adopted "dram shop" acts, making it illegal to sell to either intoxicated persons or minors. The nature and scope of these acts vary from state to state. Therefore, campus officials must carefully review statutes in their areas to insure compliance.

Some states' dram shop acts go so far as to impose penalties regardless of the seller's knowledge of the purchaser's sobriety or age. Such statutes place a strict duty on the seller to determine a purchaser's age or condition prior to sale or distribution. On campus, such responsibility could crop up in many situations, including sporting events, fund-raising activities, and student social gatherings.

STRICT LIABILITY

Many states have taken traditional dram shop provisions a step further: They impose civil liability on the seller or provider for any injuries resulting from the illegal purchaser's use. Under these statutes, wrongful sale of alcohol, plus resulting injury, equals the seller's liability — no questions asked. Where these tough laws apply, schools that sell alcohol have to make sure they're not selling to people who're underage or already drunk. If they don't, they'll find themselves in a tort liability situation with no available defense.

Not all states have legislated civil liability for alcohol-servers. But in many that haven't, the courts, in effect, have — through decisions in favor of those injured by illegal drinkers. One way they've done this is by finding that violation of criminal laws related to furnishing alcohol is in fact negligence — meaning tort law is then applicable.

A few states have entirely resisted pressure to go the dram shop route. For example, see *Bell v. Alpha Tau Omega Fraternity*, 642 P.2d 161 (Nevada 1982).

Indeed, in some states courts and legislatures are at odds on the issue. Where court-imposed liability has been expanded, some legislatures have responded by acting to protect sellers. Two factors contribute to this legislative response: (1) the casualty insurance crisis, and (2) the powerful retail alcohol lobby. Retailers unable to buy enough insurance have pushed for more state protection, while the liquor lobby has promoted limiting or eliminating dram shop liability.

However, this type of debate ignores the public-health impact of dram shop laws. Dram shop liability, properly applied, is important to preventing alcohol-related injuries. Lobbying groups in the debate generally promote their own interests, not the public interest.

The strict liability created by dram shop provisions makes it important that all schools involved in the sale or distribution of alcohol become familiar with applicable local and state law. Much of the attention in the past several years has focused on social hosts. (And with good reason — the law has been rapidly changing in this area.) However, those selling alcohol have a much greater level of liability and must take precautions to manage that risk.

This means that schools must see to it that they have firm control of the way liquor is sold on their campuses. Colleges and universities that sell alcohol are bound by the prevailing standards of tort law — reasonable care to prevent foreseeable risks.

PREVENTIVE MEDICINE

Colleges and universities continue to sell alcohol on campus, and will continue to do so in the future. To provide maximum protection from dram shop liability, and to protect people, they should adopt responsible business practices, such as:

- Designated Driver or Shuttle Service. Groups designate one or more members to stay "sober" during certain events for the purpose of transporting intoxicated guests home. Drivers should check to make sure that their insurance covers this situation. To off-campus events, some form of shuttle service can be an effective method of reducing risks.

- Provision for Non-Alcoholic Beverages. Provide plenty of non-alcoholic beverages. Try to have the same quantity and variety of non-alcoholic and alcoholic beverages to allow social guests to make an uninhibited choice.

- Serving Food. Make sure that plenty of food is available at all events. Good food can draw some attention away from alcohol.

- Checking Identification. A basic point, but one that always needs to be emphasized: check for proper identification and reject questionable forms of ID. Legal problems, including civil and criminal liability, are made more serious when an aggressive policy of restricting service of alcohol to those of legal age is not pursued by student groups or organizations.

- Discouraging Self-Service of Alcoholic Beverages. Organization members or hired bartenders should be used whenever possible to limit the size of drinks being served and spot those who are drinking too much.

- Posting Drinking Restrictions in Prominent Places. Notices containing information on legal drinking age should be posted at entrances to alcohol events and at interior locations where alcohol is actually being served.

- Restricting Alcohol to a Controlled Area. Don't allow alcohol out of a controlled area. Insure that it is consumed or disposed of by all participants before they leave the premises. Campus or organizational responsibility can easily travel with drinks that travel.

- Limiting or Eliminating References to Alcohol in Advertisements. Pictures of beer kegs and mugs will not help anyone's defense in a legal action. Keep references to the type and quantity of alcohol to be served out of promotional materials. Don't use alcohol as the draw for the event. Stay away from "Drink and Drown" or "Beer Blast" themes. Emphasize the nature of the event, not the alcohol.

- Limiting Hours of Alcohol Service. Make sure that alcohol service is stopped at a reasonable time, at least an hour or so before an event is scheduled to end. It also helps to post the closing time near the bar to avoid misunderstandings at the end of an event.

- Promotion of Activities Other Than Drinking. Don't make people drink because they have nothing else to do at a campus event. Encourage other activities, like dancing, to help break down social barriers without alcohol.

- Making Sure Applicable Requirements Are Complied With. If permits or licenses are required, make sure they are obtained. Adhere to all campus, local, and state standards.

- Not Serving Intoxicated Guests. Instead, diplomatically ask for their car keys and offer to drive them home. The risks are too great to take any other action. If the event sponsors spot someone who has exceeded his or her limit, additional alcohol should not be served to that person and a reasonable effort should be made to arrange for a safe trip home.

There is no perfect system for eliminating the potential for liability when alcohol is served. However, where alcohol is made available, those providing it have a responsibility to do all that can be done to limit the risks — of harm and liability — for everyone's sake.

States Put Crunch on Colleges for Unfair Business Competition

In recent years, commercial businesses have become increasingly concerned over alleged taxpayer-supported unfair competition by not-for-profit organizations, like colleges and universities.

The conflict between campus enterprises and community entrepreneurs is easy to understand, if not solve. Local businesses complain that colleges and universities should be in the "education" business, instead of joining the private sector in providing things like computers, food service, housing, travel services, bookstores, medical services, and sweatshirts. Small businesses deeply resent what they have quickly come to perceive as unfair competition.

The merchants' voice of complaint has not gone entirely unheeded. The concerns of small businesses have sometimes been heard at the campus level — where limited reforms have been made. They're being heard in courtrooms — but the issue has proven difficult for the courts to define and decide. It's being reviewed at the state level — where legislation has been enacted or is pending in dozens of states. And at the federal level, the issue has been heard, but left unanswered. As more and more colleges look at the need to generate additional support revenues, the limiting implications of local business concerns will have to be considered — at all levels.

The federal Small Business Administration studied the issue extensively, and published "Unfair Competition by Non-Profit Organizations with Small Businesses: An Issue for the 1980s" in 1984.

The SBA report contended that a non-profit institution, like a college, is in fact a commercial enterprise if it gets most of its funding from sales or fees, rather than grants or donations. This restrictive definition would place most colleges, hospitals, and museums, regardless of status or sponsorship, in the category of commercial enterprises. If that definition was widely adopted, competitive advantages of non-profits — including federal and state tax exemptions, exemptions from property taxes, and favorable postal rates — could be lost.

Many see the unrelated business tax as the obvious tool with which to battle non-profits that compete with commercial businesses. Non-profit organizations, which are generally tax-exempt, must pay a tax on any income unrelated to their principal activity. The tax is assessed at the same rate that a commercial vendor would pay, and is designed to prevent unfair competition. In the past, the government and courts have interpreted "unrelated business" rather loosely, allowing non-profits wide latitude in their income-generating activities.

However, as charges of unfair competition increase, stricter standards for unrelated business income are developing. These tougher standards make the tax a real threat to some colleges and universities heavily engaged in alternative income-producing activities.

One group with a naturally strong interest in the situation, the National Association of College and University Business Officers, has attempted to head off conflicts by drafting guidelines for members. These call for limiting campus profit-making ventures to activities that *fulfill an integral role in the school mission*, plus services needed on campus. They stress the need for sensitivity on the issue of commercial endeavors, advocating a balancing between community and university interests.

Today, as federal consideration of colleges' business income has apparently stalled, state legislatures are actively pursuing the question. Upon examining some of the recent state-level solutions to this problem, it looks like the threatened federal tax action would have been an easier pill for higher education to swallow.

CAMPUS AND COURT

Some campuses are trying to deal with the issue on their own, now rather than later. These administrations hope campus solutions can reduce the need for less sensitive government guidelines. Establishing *advisory councils* to meet and discuss areas of concern is a good first step in dealing with this important town-gown problem. Typically, schools get together with local industry councils or chambers of commerce to form such panels to serve in an advisory capacity. By sharing information and plans — and developing an understanding of individual and mutual needs — some problems can be averted. Through improved communication channels, better understanding of the needs of all parties is possible.

Courtroom airings of the issue are becoming more common. The issues of conference use of residence halls, sale of computers, and sale of hearing aids have all been tested in court in the last few years:

Outside groups may still use the dormitories at Southern Oregon State College, despite a legal conflict stretching over many years between the school and local businesses. Computer sales practices at the University of Illinois have changed since an unfair-competition lawsuit against the school several years ago. The school used to run a computer store on campus; no longer. Facing bitter complaints from local private computer vendors, the school stopped the practice and entered into a sales arrangement that included, not competed with, local vendors.

In Arizona and Alabama, the issue was hearing aid sales to patients in campus clinics. Fitting the aids was part of students' educational program, and the sales took place on campus for patient convenience and so that all students would be fitting the same model. In Arizona, local businessmen successfully blocked university sales of hearing aids. However, in Alabama, the same facts led to an opposite result: Sale of the devices was judged appropriate for the school, given the educational context. In court, the argument that a campus activity is in *some* way educational is hard to beat. Courts have understandably had difficulty drawing a clear line between "What is education?" and "What is business?"

THE STATEHOUSES

The level of concern over the business-campus controversy has risen highest in the state legislatures in recent years. Many states have adopted, or are considering, statutes designed to *eliminate*, not just limit competition between higher education and industry. Before 1988, four states had passed laws addressing unfair competition, and at least three more joined the bandwagon that year. State legislation so far has taken three basic forms: (1) study commissions and review boards; (2) restriction or elimination of competitive sales; and (3) mandated adoption of internally developed policies by non-profit competitors.

Arizona and Louisiana took the first route, establishing review boards and grievance procedures to deal with complaints and new-enterprise proposals. Washington state lawmakers considered a variety of proposals aimed at unfair business competition, but for the time being have settled on allowing individual campuses to develop internal policies on the matter. Illinois was the first to take the tough restrictive route — requiring regular reporting from state agencies and banning competitive sales by state agencies, including public universities. In 1988, Iowa, Idaho, and Colorado followed suit, adopting laws banning sales that compete with private enterprise or don't fulfill a mission of the institution.

The trend toward further, similarly restrictive state legislation is clear; and the impact on campus could be enormous.

THE FEDS

At the federal level, solutions are not as clear. The House Ways and Means Committee's Oversight subcommittee was expected to make a recommendation on the issue of *unrelated business income* in 1988. After two years of consideration, it appears the issue remains unsettled in committee.

The federal method of dealing with the unfair competition problem is through the tax code. Revenues generated by not-for-profit institutions are not taxed if they relate to the performance of the institution's purpose, or are conducted for the convenience of the institutional population. In other words, a non-profit may generate revenues not for the mission or for institutional convenience, but those revenues are taxable. Universities must pay taxes on unrelated income over $1,000.

The Ways and Means Committee, responding to small businesses, was expected to toughen the standards for exempt income in 1988. This step alone would not prevent what some see as unfair competition, but it would tax more such efforts by higher education institutions. However, Congress is not able, or not yet willing, to deal with what many consider an abuse of institutional not-for-profit status.

College and university administrators will continue to feel pressure in coming years over business competition and unrelated business income — at the local, state, and federal levels *and* in the courts. Some difficult questions will get answered during this time: Do the offered goods and services truly promote the mission of the institution? Even if they do promote the mission, is it fair to use the school name or facilities to compete with local private business? While colleges' search for more financial support is very understandable in today's economic environment, questions over unrelated business and unfair competition will not go away.

Without quick attention to the problem at the local level, this issue may be decided by the states — and that decision could take the form of a ban on such activities. Schools should consider the consequences of provoking such a ban when framing their town-gown relations on this issue.

Principles

- Any residence hall billing system should resort to group billing only after every effort has been made to identify the individuals actually responsible for damage.

- Student service corporations, like other corporations, are accountable to the directors, the membership, the campus, and the community.

- The strict liability created by dram shop laws makes it important that all schools involved in the sale or distribution of alcohol become familiar with applicable local and state law.

- The National Association of College and University Business Officers recommends limiting campus profit-making ventures (other than those supplying needed campus services) to activities that fulfill an integral role in the school mission.

4. Academic Issues

It is the business of a university to provide that atmosphere which is most conducive to speculation, experiment and creation. It is an atmosphere in which there prevail 'the four essential freedoms' of a university — to determine for itself on academic grounds who may teach, what may be taught, how it shall be taught, and who may be admitted to study.
— *Sweezy v. New Hampshire* (Frankfurter, J., concurring), 354 U.S. at 263 (1956), quoting *The Open Universities in South Africa* (conference report)

Academic freedom is one of the best-established doctrines in higher education law. The general judicial approach to purely academic matters is, in a word, hands-off.

But that doesn't mean the courts keep their noses out of academics; after all, how many things are "purely" academic? The line blurs at the racial barrier, as in *Regents of University of California v. Bakke*, 438 U.S. 265 (1978); in the counselor's office; in the giving of standardized tests; and in the field (internships and cooperative education). Herein we look closely at some of those fuzzy demarcations.

Academic Decisions and the Courts

When can students sue over bad grades and on what grounds? A new case involving a student at the University of Northern Iowa brings the issue back into the legal spotlight.

The student's first attempt at legal action was dismissed by a judge who ruled that the court lacked jurisdiction in areas of academic discretion. But now, the student, who sued a professor after a disagreement over a bad grade, will be given a new trial. In ordering that the case be heard again, however, the Iowa Supreme Court did not address the issue of whether the issuance of a grade is a discretionary matter. Besides asking for a review of the grade, the student's suit claimed he was entitled to actual and punitive damages due to "willful and malicious acts performed" by the professor with intent to damage him.

Traditionally, courts have paid more attention to issues of student conduct outside the classroom than they have to their academic experience. Courts have felt ill at ease looking over professors' shoulders. As the decision in *Board of Curators of the University of Missouri v. Horowitz*, 435 U.S 78 (1978), puts it: "Courts are particularly ill-equipped to evaluate academic performance." A fuller explanation of this principle, and student grounds for challenges to it, can be found in an earlier case, *Connolly v. University of Vermont*, 244 F.Supp. 156 (1965):

"In matters of scholarship, the school authorities are uniquely qualified by training and experience to judge the qualifications of a student, and efficiency of instruction depends in no small degree upon the school's faculty's freedom from interference from other noneducational tribunals. It is only when the school authorities abuse this discretion that a court may interfere with their decision."

In general, student attempts to have courts review grading decisions must include a showing that school officials have acted arbitrarily or have abused the discretionary authority vested in them.

The terms of the "contract" between students and the institution may also be used to find a basis for legal action. "The terms and conditions ... are those offered by the publications of the college at the time of enrollment ... and have some of the characteristics of a contract," allowing for challenges based on possible breaches of that contract in grading decisions.

In recent years, claims of sexual harassment have added a new ground for grading reviews. In a 1980 case, five female students at Yale University sought court review of campus policies for dealing with sexual harassment. They claimed Yale was in violation of Title IX of the Education Amendments of 1972. Title IX generally requires that on the basis of sex, no one can "be excluded from participation in, be denied the benefits of, or be subjected to discrimination under any education program or activity" receiving federal funds. The Yale students alleged that a faculty member had offered a grade of A in exchange for compliance with sexual demands. The case — *Alexander v. Yale University*, 631 F.2d 178 (1980) — also made allegations of other instances of sexual harassment and inadequate campus-response procedures.

The U.S. District Court and U.S. Court of Appeals decided the case in favor of Yale, but in doing so specifically noted that a review of grades was a "justifiable claim" under Title IX. In *Alexander*, the allegations were found speculative and uncertain, but other cases of this type, supported by evidence, were encouraged by courts that traditionally have not sought review of grade-related matters.

In the recent University of Northern Iowa lawsuit, the student claims that he received an F in a biostatistics class after he and the professor had a disagreement over work done for the course. The suit states that the student threw away a computer statement on the advice of another instructor. As a result, the biostatistics professor became angry, argued with the student, and asked him to drop the course. The student reportedly agreed to leave the class but refused to turn in his homework — a data deck designed for class use. The suit contends that the professor called the student "stupid," threatened to have him thrown off campus, and claimed he would be barred from campus in the future.

In addition to a court review of the F, the suit seeks $35,000 in actual damages and $100,000 in punitive damages from the University of Northern Iowa and the state of Iowa.

In the light of past court decisions in similar matters, it's clear a supported showing of bad faith, arbitrariness, or a violation of the student-institutional contract will be needed to obtain judicial intrusion into this and other instances of academic decision-making, since courts are unwilling to substitute their judgment for that of instructors or administrators on issues of academic concern. The University of Northern Iowa can look east to find further support for this principle. In *McIntosh v. Borough of Manhattan Community College*, 449 N.Y.S.2d 26 (1982), a state court refused to get involved in a class grade dispute.

In a case involving the rounding-off of grades, the court reiterated what we already knew: Don't come to them unless you can prove a violation of due process or a decision that is arbitrary or capricious.

Bad Advice Can End Up in Court

What happens when a student who completes his course of study suddenly hears: "There's been a mistake; there's more work to do"?

What if an instructor misinforms the class on grading procedures for an exam, causing students to spend too much time on the wrong sections? Can these kinds of issues wind up in court?

Advisement questions do make it to court fairly regularly. At issue is the advice or information provided by staff or faculty. If a student misinterprets the information, or the information is in fact wrong, the legal system may decide responsibility and assess damages.

Courts often apply contract theory to the situation. They find that an agreement was made, and each party is bound to uphold its side of the bargain.

In *Healy v. Larsson*, 323 N.Y.S.2d 625, the court found that academic advisement was in fact contractual. A student at a community college had spent a great deal of time, prior to enrollment, planning his academic program with several knowledgeable faculty and staff members. When he completed the arranged course work, the college denied him a degree, saying that he hadn't taken the proper courses. The student argued unsuccessfully with the college that he'd completed what all had agreed should be done. He then took it to court.

The court found there was a contract between the school and student in the academic advice the staff and faculty had given him. When a student completes the courses the school instructs him to take, he is entitled to the appropriate degree. Additional requirements can't be imposed at that point. This application of contract law to advisement is valid at both private and public institutions, in the view of the courts.

IN CLASS

Similar problems of misunderstanding or misinformation can occur in the classroom. What happens when an instructor gives wrong grading information to students before an important exam? In *Olsson v. Board of Higher Education*, 426 N.Y.S.2d 248, an instructor during a review session misled the class on how the papers would be graded. After the exam, a student who failed under the grading system in force, but who would have passed if papers were marked as the instructor had told them, demanded a passing grade.

The student claimed he would have spent his exam time more wisely if he had known the true grading policy. The school refused to change the grade and denied the student a degree as a result. The school did offer him a chance to retake the exam, but he refused. The matter then headed for the courts.

The trial court ruled in the student's favor, saying the school must award a degree if the student satisfies the criteria for completing courses and degree work. The court held that this principle applies even when the wrong criteria are communicated, and as a result the student satisfies the wrong level of achievement.

On appeal, however, the higher court reversed in favor of the school. At issue, they held, was the integrity of academic degrees: Awarding a degree implies that a student has met certain levels of academic achievement. People must be able to trust in the value of degrees, and degrees which are unearned make the value of all degrees subject to question. (Courts should only become involved in the process when there is evidence that an institution has acted arbitrarily and unreasonably, the court added.)

In the offer of a make-up examination, the court found a good-faith effort to correct the instructor's misstatement. This offer was a reasonable solution and one that preserved both the student's rights and academic integrity.

In light of court decisions which give contract status to advisement, consider the following when reviewing advisement procedures for possible legal difficulties:

- Restrict advice-giving to those qualified to provide proper advisement.
- Clearly communicate to students where official advice can be obtained, to avoid problems of apparent authority.
- Where regulations require institutions to notify students of academic progress, follow the regulations.
- Even where not required, officials are wise to keep students advised of difficulties which may affect degree eligibility.
- Schools do not have a duty to warn students who are unlikely to successfully complete an academic program.
- Review college catalogs and bulletins to remove any ambiguities.

Institutions and instructors clearly need to be able to provide academic advice. They should take care, however, to insure that the advice is accurate, for the sake of the student and the institution. The consequences of error are often found in the courtroom.

Standardized Tests: Necessary, Evil, or Both?

Use of educational ability and achievement tests — in admissions, graduation, and employment processes — has greatly expanded in the past decade, but the validity and value of standardized testing is under attack on and off campus.

The growth of testing, in part, reflects increasing concern over the quality of higher education in America. Better monitoring of the quality of individuals seeking admission to colleges and universities, and better testing of students before graduation, are common suggestions for improving the situation.

Many schools have taken those suggestions. But increased use of educational testing raises important legal issues. In addition, the testing of graduates' qualifications for hiring purposes has campus implications. Higher education, as it tests *and is tested* more, must be aware of these legal issues related to admissions testing, minimum-competence tests, and so on.

Those who rely on computerized testing in admissions, graduation, and employment decisions should keep one eye on the law. As a first step, read the following. Note that many standardized-testing cases that focus on important legal issues have cropped up at the elementary- and secondary-school levels. However, the lessons learned from legal decisions in those settings often apply to colleges and universities.

LEGAL STANDARDS

The obligation to be fair in standardized testing derives both from the Constitution and from legislation. Many standards of testing fairness relate to prohibited *discrimination*.

As with most higher education law, the status of the institution — private or public — determines what standards apply. When there is "state action," the constitutional protections of due process and equal protection are enforceable. State action is in the picture when standardized testing takes place at or for a public college or university.

For private schools, legislation dealing with fairness and fair processes is applicable, not the due process and equal protection clauses. Federal laws with educational-testing implications include: Title VI of the Civil Rights Act of 1964; Title IX of the 1972 Education Amendments; Section 504 of the Rehabilitation Act of 1973; the Equal Opportunity Act of 1974; the Family Educational Rights and Privacy Act of 1974; and the Age Discrimination Act of 1975. (On top of these federal acts, many states have adopted truth-in-testing laws and sunshine laws that can affect campus testing.)

THE BASES FOR CHALLENGE

Legal challenges to testing increase in direct proportion to increases in the amount of testing. Issues that regularly come up in cases against standardized educational tests and testing procedures include:

- due process concerns,
- allegations of built-in cultural bias, and
- confidentiality problems.

Courts have found a lack of *substantive due process* where tests cover materials not taught. In *Anderson v. Banks*, 520 F.Supp. 472 (1981), the court sided with opponents of the California Achievement Test (CAT) as a measure of reading and math competence for high school graduation. The court ruled that a test must be "curricularly valid" — meaning that it must test only materials taught if it measures graduation readiness.

Procedural due process problems have also shown up in minimum-competence examination challenges. In Texas, the courts enjoined use of a test for approved college and university teacher-education programs. The challenge was filed both by students who did not want to take the competence exam and by those who failed it. The court found preliminary merit in these arguments:

- the test had a discriminatory intent that violated *equal protection* rights
- there was inadequate notice of the time and need for testing, violating *due process* standards
- the test would result in illegal *discrimination* from a program receiving federal funds, in violation of Title VI of the Civil Rights Act of 1964
- the exam was a result of the state's denying *equal education opportunity* due to race, in violation of the Equal Educational Opportunity Act of 1974.

A Florida high school minimum-competence reading examination also drew a challenge on equal protection grounds. Black students in segregated schools claimed they did not have adequate notice of what the test would cover, and did not have time to prepare. The Fifth Circuit U.S. Court of Appeals ruled the test was valid, in that it tested appropriate materials, but delayed implementation of the test until all the students had gone through desegregated schools — that is, for 12 years.

The court, in *Debra P. v. Turlington*, 474 F.Supp 244 (1979), 644 F.2d 397 (1981), concluded — based on fundamental fairness — that the students must have a chance to be fully taught the materials tested.

Confidentiality concerns surfaced in *Wood v. National Computer Systems, Inc.*, 643 F.Supp 1093 (1986). An Arkansas public school teacher sued a company hired to do testing for invasion of privacy and infliction of emotional distress. Reason: The company had sent her test scores to the wrong person. The court agreed with her in principle, saying test results should be protected under the Family Education Rights and Privacy Act. (Test scores have been considered educational records under the law.) That act has the effect of limiting test-score access to students and those they authorize. (See page 48 for more about FERPA.) In this case, however, the court concluded that while the test scores should have been better protected, the plaintiff's giving television interviews on the matter negated her claims of invasion of privacy and distress.

Cultural bias was the charge against an IQ test used for admissions purposes in public schools in California. The much-publicized case, *Larry P. v. Riles*, 343 F.Supp. 1306 (1972), 48 USLW 2298 (1979), featured the claim that the test was culturally biased against black children. Challengers argued this violated the children's constitutional and statutory rights. Evidence included statements that the standardized test was developed on an all-white population. The dispute finally produced an order prohibiting use of standardized IQ tests for black students in the state.

ON CAMPUS

As colleges and universities look for better ways to evaluate academic acceptability and achievement, the trend toward increased standardized testing will continue. Avoid problems: Evaluate your campus' admissions, placement, and degree testing to make sure:

- adequate notice of requirements is provided.
- adequate time and opportunity for preparation in advance of testing is provided.
- tests cover only the materials taught.
- tests are not culturally biased.
- access to test results is restricted to only those authorized.

The Legal Ingredients of Internships

Every day, colleges and universities across the country send students off campus to pursue education and experience. Internships, career development programs, and so on provide students with undeniable educational value: real work environments, hands-on training and skill development, and better preparation for the job market.

However, institutions participating in (and often, arranging) these programs must know the very real legal problems that accompany off-campus connections. That way, schools can better plan, implement, and evaluate internship and cooperative education programs to both maximize the student's experience and minimize the college's risk. Some of the obvious legal hazards for participating schools:

- breach of contract
- student injuries or death, and
- violation of education and labor laws.

A CONTRACT IS A CONTRACT

Contractual problems can spring from several quarters: failure to meet a student's expectations; changes in existing academic programs aimed at meeting internship or cooperative-education needs; failure of the student or program to satisfy the employer's needs.

The key to meeting student expectations lies in making sure that the materials students get are clear and accurate. The information they receive should specifically establish the program's goals and methods, and identify expected outcomes. Make sure all university documents related to off-campus programs are accurate and consistent.

The other side of this coin is to share the same information with the employers or sponsors involved — whether public or private. The employers have expectations too, and their understanding of the relationship between the school and the off-campus program is important in setting those expectations.

As always, university documents for this purpose should state that the school reserves the right to alter or eliminate the program as needed under specific conditions. If such a need does arise, more is necessary: Schools modifying or terminating courses or programs should be ready to demonstrate the legitimate need for that action.

Successful internship or cooperative education programs can affect faculty and staff resources. Implementing a program, or supporting a program's implementation or enhancement, may mean reallocating existing staff and funding. When this happens, administrators must consider the possibility of lawsuits by staff. The potential is also there for a legal response from students whose academic programs are changed or scrapped due to resource shifts.

Institutions considering such reallocations must review existing contracts and procedures to make sure they are looking out for faculty and student rights.

Employers or sponsors may also have a contractual right of action against a school — for instance, where the school fails to provide the type of student the employer needs, or where the student doesn't perform as promised. If the employer or sponsoring organization suffers because of the student's acts or omissions, it could seek payment for breach of contract.

Therefore, it is crucial that the college and the sponsoring organizations clearly establish and understand all parties' rights, responsibilities, and legal limitations before entering into any internship program.

LOOKING OUT FOR THEIR SAFETY

The normal concern that an institution has for its students' safety is even greater when students participate in school-sponsored, off-campus programs or events. For one thing, there is danger of student injury or death off campus.

Second, in general, the greater the school's role in supervising the internship, the higher the risk of being held responsible for off-campus incidents. Put another way, the school's "duty to care" increases as school supervision of the experience increases.

One way to evaluate off-campus risks is to conduct inspections of internship work places. University staff can do this effectively if the inspections are properly designed (and the staff properly trained) to assess placement-site hazards. However, on-site inspection programs, besides using resources, raise legal questions: By examining a site and certifying its safety, the school creates a higher degree of liability for incidents there.

A signed release or consent form may be a more reasonable approach. These forms do not completely bar legal action or recovery. But they are useful to show that students fully understood the off-campus risks, and made an informed decision to participate. Forms for this purpose should specifically deal with internship or cooperative education programs, and should make clear to participants that the school has not inspected the site in advance. In addition, the form should advise students that they must evaluate the safety of the work site before accepting the position.

Clearly state any attempt to eliminate or limit responsibility for off-campus placement incidents.

In reviewing the validity of release or consent forms, courts always look at the relative bargaining position of the parties to make sure the signer freely and knowingly released the other from liability. Therefore, it is important for schools using these forms to make clear to students that they are free to reject, without academic or financial penalty, any unsafe or risky assignment.

One other area to consider in avoiding liability for accidents or injuries: school release of student medical records. It is important to advise sponsors and employers in advance of participants' medical conditions that could put them or others at risk of injury. Therefore, get authorization from participating students to release individual medical information when appropriate.

If a student does not allow release of the information, the institution should consider placing her in a safer program environment, or withdrawing her entirely from the program. When a student's condition puts her or others at risk in an off-campus placement, and the school has relevant medical information it doesn't share, the institution is greatly increasing its exposure to liability and damages.

STAYING WITHIN THE LAW

In addition to meeting expectations and assessing safety, schools must insure that internships and work-study programs are in compliance with applicable state and federal higher-education and labor laws.

A student's status as employee or intern has a bearing on matters such as compensation and benefits. Also, institutions should make sure all potential placement sites comply with applicable civil rights standards: Request an acknowledgement that they do not discriminate on the basis of race, sex, age, or handicap, and that the work area is reasonably accessible to handicapped students. A school's failure to insist on sponsor or employer civil rights compliance could create an opportunity for federal or state action against the institution — for sponsoring illegally discriminatory programs.

Given the contractual, safety, and legal implications of student internships and cooperative education placements, colleges and universities must carefully evaluate all programs of this type. Because any off-campus placement carries increased risk, make sure that careful controls of the liability risks accompany these horizon-broadening opportunities.

Principles

- It is only when school authorities abuse their discretion to judge the qualifications of a student that the courts may interfere with their decision.

- Restrict academic advice-giving to those qualified to provide proper advisement.

- Institutions and instructors should take care to insure that academic advice is accurate.

- The obligation to be fair in standardized testing derives both from the Constitution and from legislation.

- It is crucial that the college and the sponsoring organizations clearly establish and understand all parties' rights, responsibilities, and legal limitations before entering into any internship program.

- Schools must insure that internships and work-study programs are in compliance with applicable state and federal higher-education and labor laws.

5. Records and Contracts

It is apparent that *some* elements of the law of contracts are used and should be used in the analysis of the relationship between [the student] and the University ... This does not mean that "contract law" must be rigidly applied in all its aspects ... The student-university relationship is unique, and it should not be and cannot be stuffed into one doctrinal category.

— *Slaughter v. Brigham Young University*, 514 F.2d at 626 (1975)

It's clear enough from what we've seen so far that any attempt at such "stuffing" would be futile. In fact, the problem is how *many* different legal doctrines affect higher education law.

In *Slaughter*, the leeway given academic freedom — and the flexibility of the courts' doctrinal application in higher education cases — once again shows through clearly. However, our advice is not to count on the law's flexibility. When it comes to records and contracts, be ready for the worst.

Study the items below, for starters: overviews of contract law and the contractual nature of the student-school relationship; a look at the current status of the Family Educational Rights and Privacy Act (Buckley Amendment) on educational records and their release; and studies of the law of duplication in the context of the computer revolution, and the elaborate financial aid maze.

What's In a Contract?

" In addition to the contract, the salesman said ... " "Along with the band, the agent promised ... " "The printer promised he would throw in ... "

Whenever there's a meeting or conference on higher education and the law, educators, administrators, and students inevitably pose a host of questions that begin with these and similar phrases. They all relate to problems that occur when a written contract between a school or a student organization and an outside speaker, vendor, or contractor doesn't contain all the agreed-upon terms.

In interpreting and enforcing a contract, questions often arise as to whether the written instrument is the complete embodiment of the parties' intention. Where the parties to a contract put their agreement in writing as a full expression of their bargain, any other expressions — written or oral — made prior to or at the same time as the written contract are inadmissible in a court battle to vary the terms of the final written contract. This is called the "Parol Evidence Rule," and it is more a rule of contract law than of evidence. It seeks to establish a single, clean source of proof on the terms of the bargain — the written contract. All outside materials — written and verbal — are deemed to be outside of the agreement, unless incorporated in the written contract.

As examples, efforts to enforce the earlier "promises" of the salesman, agent, or printer beyond what was agreed to in writing in the final contract would be difficult. The court will look at what is written, and presume it is the complete agreement.

Say student organization "A" has negotiated to buy a new photocopy machine from company "B." The salesman for "B" tells the group before or as they sign the sales agreement that as a bonus, he will "throw in" some extra paper and supplies beyond those called for in the contract. The machine arrives but without paper and supplies.

Can group "A" get salesman "B" to perform as he promised? Can "A" enforce the full agreement, including the extra supplies and paper? Probably not, due to the Parol Evidence Rule. The court would review the written agreement and presume it says all the parties intended to say on the matter. Other evidence of further agreements would generally be excluded, unless used to show "fraud in the inducement" of the contract. (*Pioneer Contractors V. Symes*, 77 Ariz. 107, 267 P.2d 740, 41 A.L.R.2d 668.)

Some other thoughts on dealing with contracts:

- Contracts are generally viewed as being "whole"; specific clauses that go against the general intent of the contract will be subordinated.

- Where provisions appear to be inconsistent, the courts will determine whether some provisions are printed (indicating a form contract) as compared to other terms or conditions which are typed or written. The typed or written provisions usually prevail.

- When there is a question of custom or usage, the court first looks to the particular business and the particular locale where the contract is to be performed.

Remember: Most courts will try to reach a determination that a contract is valid and enforceable. They tend to view contract provisions in a manner that makes the contract "operative" unless this would contravene the intention of the parties.

When dealing with written contracts, the following common-sense approach can help in avoiding Parol Evidence Rule problems:

- Read the contract completely.

- Check to see that any blanks are filled in appropriately.

- Ask questions.

- Make sure you understand the answers.

- Does the written contract contain all the agreed-upon points?

- Does the contract say what happens if there is a dispute over the terms or language?

- Does all the language adequately describe the terms in such a way that a third person (i.e., a judge) will clearly understand the intentions of the parties?

- Is the term of the agreement correctly noted? Is there a renewal process?

- Have all appendices attached or referred to been reviewed?

- Has legal counsel been consulted wherever and whenever appropriate?

Every day, colleges and universities, faculty, staff, and students sign thousands of agreements. A proper contract can protect everyone's interest. Make sure that everything is in writing and understood by everyone.

Copyright Law Catches Up
with the Computer Age

The mushrooming of campus microcomputer use has spawned a variety of software issues and controversies for colleges and universities. Most of the legal difficulties relate to acquisition and use of software: illegal copying, multiple copies, preview, and networking. The 1976 Copyright Act and its computer amendment answered some of the basic questions — but schools still need to adopt software policies covering purchase, preview, and use of protected materials. They also need to educate students on the ethical dimensions of software use.

A copyright gives to the author of a protected product the exclusive right to make copies of that product. He can sell his copyright, or transfer it, to a person or an organization. Therefore, the producer of a software product controls the fate of that program.

The law does give the buyer of a software package some rights as well. The buyer can make a backup copy of a protected program to protect it against human or machine damage. In addition, the sales or lease agreement between producer and purchaser may establish other rights or limitations.

In a lease arrangement, the parties specifically agree on uses and a time period for use. Neither side can violate those provisions. While a legitimate user of a leased program is legally entitled to a backup program, there is no legal consensus on who should provide the copy. Some producers include one in the lease package for an additional fee; others (presumably) permit the user to make necessary copies, if none are provided.

In a sale, the buyer can make as many back-up copies of the program as necessary. A purchase plan does not, however, permit a purchaser to make copies of the software and distribute them to other potential users.

The fair use doctrine of the Copyright Act permits copying and use of small portions of programs for teaching, research, and scholarship purposes. It does not allow an instructor to make a complete copy of a program for academic purposes. Just as you can't copy a complete book or film, you can't make an unauthorized copy of a complete computer program. No set amount of copying constitutes a "fair" amount. Therefore, copy only that portion of a program necessary for a specific educational purpose.

Institutions can reduce their liability for illegal copying of disks by means similar to those used to reduce illegal photocopying risks:

- Display a sign near computers stating that duplication of a copy of copyrighted materials is illegal.

- If there is reason to believe that illegal copies are being made, withhold university-controlled protected programs and equipment from the individuals involved.

- Require users of protected materials to sign statements to the effect that they will comply with copyright laws.

- Educate students about legal and ethical problems that result from illegal software use.

- Purchase or lease software from authorized agencies.

- Read, understand, and sign software license agreements.

As a means of enforcing illegal-copying policies, the International Council for Computers in Education recommends that schools not extend legal or insurance protection to employees who violate copyright laws. In an infringement case, both school and instructor would be sued, under normal circumstances. The ICCE proposal would leave an instructor found in violation of copyright law high and dry — without school-provided legal protection.

Computer law is growing rapidly. Legal decisions over the next few years are expected to reinforce basic principles of copyright law. College and university software users, and administrators, should make certain that they establish and follow legally reasonable policies on software acquisition and use — to avoid becoming a test case.

Important Regulations Clarify
Buckley Amendment

The U.S. Dept. of Education has finalized new regulations interpreting the Family Educational Rights and Privacy Act (FERPA) of 1974 (20 U.S.C., sec. 1232g) — popularly known as the Buckley Amendment. The new regulations cover these significant areas: release of records from other institutions; directory information; education vs. employment records; waiver of rights; and waivers to provide services. Interpretation language has been added to each area to clarify confusing points in the original legislation and implementing regulations (34 C.F.R., part 99).

The Buckley Amendment established a strong role for the federal government in college and university management and use of student records. It applies to *all* schools, public and private, that receive or use funding from the Education Dept. In cases where state laws on student records conflict with the language of FERPA, an institution has a choice between complying with FERPA or losing federal financial support.

THE BASICS OF BUCKLEY

The Act governs the *right of access* to educational records, and is designed to protect students' and parents' privacy regarding school records. Any student enrolled, or formerly enrolled, in a higher education institution has rights under the law.

Parents have a right to records until a student reaches 18; then the right passes to the student — unless the student is dependent, for income tax purposes, on the parents. In that case, *both* the student and the parents have rights under the Act. Applicants for admission to a school do *not* have FERPA rights, since they are not "students" by the Act's definition.

FERPA and its implementing regulations established policies on:
- Student access to education records
- Students' rights to challenge information in their records
- Release of information that is "personally identifiable" to others, in or outside the school
- Students' rights to a review and investigation of complaints under the Act.

EXEMPTIONS

In general, students have a right to *all campus records that directly affect them* and are maintained by the school. Put another way, if a school-held record is "directly related to a student," the student may examine it. There are few exemptions to FERPA:

- *Private notes:* personal records of staff, maintained by the makers, and not accessible to or shared with others.
- *Employment records:* maintained for employment purposes only, and defined by state law as confidential personnel records.
- *Treatment records:* health-related records made by professionals in the course of treatment, shared only for treatment purposes. (Note: These records are closed to the student, but open to a health care professional selected by the student.)
- *Public safety records:* maintained only for law-enforcement purposes, maintained separately from other student records, and shared only with law enforcement in a given jurisdiction.
- *Alumni records:* maintained by the school, containing only information on a person from the time her student career ended.

STUDENT RIGHTS

A student has the right of access to records covered by the Act during and after enrollment. In addition to the opportunity to *view* covered files, students can request an *explanation or interpretation* of records. They also have the right to copies, where circumstances prevent personal inspection.

After examining records, a student has the right to challenge the accuracy of any information included. FERPA guidelines include a procedure for hearings, to determine if materials are inaccurate, misleading, or violate privacy. If the challenge reveals an error, the school must correct the record and inform the student or parents that the correction has been made.

If the challenged record is not adjusted, the student has the right to provide a written explanation of his position, which must be included in the record for future reviews. However, this right to explanation doesn't extend to grades and academic performance evaluations.

The Buckley Amendment's primary purpose is to maintain privacy of student records as appropriate. However, under some special circumstances, the law permits disclosure of student information without specific consent.

Directory information is an example. A school may release, without consent, a student's name, address, telephone number, date and place of birth, field of study, activities, sports (and the weight and height of athletic team members), attendance dates, degrees and awards, and other similar information. However, schools must inform students of their policy on release of directory information, and give them an opportunity to withdraw their information from directories.

Specific student records are also available without student consent under certain circumstances. School officials with a *legitimate need* to see data have access to records. Also, in the case of records which are not personally identifiable, educational authorities or organizations — federal, state, or private — have access for *research and testing* purposes. And, of course, FERPA allows release of student records in cases of health or safety emergency, or in response to lawfully issued court orders and subpoenas.

THE NEW GUIDELINES

The new Education Dept. regulations are intended to clarify policy and enforcement matters in the original Act and its implementation statute.

For one thing, the Act requires that students have access to all covered records maintained by a school, even if the records originally came from other sources such as transcripts from other schools. The new regulations make clear that while students can *review* these materials, schools do not have to *release* records from another agency to third parties (students). Also, schools are free under the Act to establish their own policies in this area — as long as they're consistently applied.

The regulations further elaborate what comes under the heading of directory information. The original list (name, address, and so on) remains intact, but the category is expanded to include any information maintained in education records that would not be seen as harmful or an invasion of privacy if released. School officials may add to directory information at their discretion; but they must inform students of changes in the policy, and give them an opportunity to have their personal information withheld.

FERPA language concerning *educational vs. employment records* has been the source of much confusion in the past decade. The new Education Dept. regulations aim to clarify the Act's intentions. If a student's employment depends on the fact that she is a student, her employment record is a campus educational record under the Act. Records of work-study, cooperative education, and teaching assistantships therefore come under the Act. If getting or keeping a job depends on, or is the result of, student status, the job record is an educational record.

Colleges and universities can have policies which permit students to waive rights they have under the Buckley Amendment. However, according to the new regulations, such waivers must be *voluntary*; and a student's failure to waive cannot be the basis for restricting her access to campus services and benefits.

Administrators should review the new Dept. of Education guidelines, to insure compliance. The Buckley Amendment has become a standard part of student-record management and use; but like other legislation, it does not remain static. Campus officials must take care to review changes in the regulations, and compare relevant state laws governing maintenance and release of records. Students' privacy rights require continued institutional awareness, concern, and appropriate conduct.

<u>For more information</u>, contact: FERPA Complaint & Information Office, Education Dept., 330 Independence Ave. SW, Washington, D.C. 20201.

Financial Aid: Understanding the Legal Aspect

The recent federal effort to link financial assistance in higher education to military draft registration has rekindled interest in the legal aspects of financial aid. The legislative joining of these two seemingly unrelated entities, and the legal test of that union, can serve as a window to the legal principles affecting financial aid and a starting point for a review of the case law in this area.

Under the Defense Dept. Appropriation Act of 1983, students desiring federal financial aid must file a statement with their school indicating compliance with the Selective Service laws. Following the lead of the federal government, many states have adopted similar legislation tying state higher-education support or admission to compliance with the Military Selective Service Act, as amended in 1982. The U.S. Supreme Court ruled on the validity of this linkage in *Selective Service System v. Minnesota Public Interest Research Group*, 104 S.Ct. 3348 (1984). The legal challenge, and enforcement efforts that followed, focused on- and off-campus attention on the *contractual, testamentary, constitutional,* and *legislative* nature of higher education financial aid.

First and foremost, financial aid is a *contract* between parties. The award of aid creates a contract between provider and recipient, subject to the basic principles of contract law.

Terms and conditions of the loan are established; limitations on use of funds or necessary academic performance are made; or conditions on post-graduation commitments may be agreed upon. For example, a court routinely upheld an agreement to perform one year of public service in exchange for a specific scholarship in *State of New York v. Coury*, 359 N.Y.S.2d 486 (1974). The court supported the state's claim to the scholarship dollars, since the former student had failed to comply with the terms of the contract.

WHERE THERE'S A WILL ...

Testamentary principles of law apply to financial aid programs established through wills and estates; similar principles affect grants and gifts. Conditions which the provider — living or dead — places on the program are to be adhered to, unless those conditions become impossible or create state action which violates non-discrimination laws.

When accomplishing the goals of a trust becomes "impossible, impracticable, or illegal ... a court ... will apply trust funds to a charitable purpose as nearly as possible to the particular purpose" that is now out of reach (*Howard Savings Institution v. Peep*, 34 N.J. 484, 170 A.2d 39 (1961)). This adaptation of the original terms of the trust to something as close as possible to it is the legal principle of *cy pres*.

In the *Howard Savings* case, Amherst College controlled a trust it could not use, because the deed of gift violated the school charter. Financial aid from the gift was to be limited to Protestants only, but the court removed that limitation (made obsolete through changing times) by applying the *cy pres* doctrine.

Using the same principle, a court dropped decades-old restrictions on class sizes from the guidelines for an aid fund in *Wilbur v. University of Vermont*, 129 Vt. 33, 270 A.2d 889 (1970). Thus, impossible, impracticable, or illegal financial-aid gift conditions are subject to modification when necessary.

Private scholarships awarded by public schools on the basis of sex came under scrutiny in *Shapiro v. Columbia Union National Bank and Trust Co.*, 576 S.W.2d 310 (1978). A trust established for "deserving Kansas City, Missouri boys" to attend the private University of Kansas City was still in place after the school became the public University of Missouri. A female law student, turned down for aid from the trust, claimed unlawful and discriminatory state action in violation of the Fourteenth Amendment and the Civil Rights Act.

The Missouri Supreme Court found that the school's handling of the trust did not violate constitutional principles: While the school processed loan applications, *private trustees made the final awards.* "We, of course, approve equal access of educational opportunity ... but this must be balanced by the right of a private person to dispose of his money or property as the testator wishes, and unless the trust is unlawful ... private trusts are to be encouraged," the court wrote.

Another single-sex private trust at a public institution was upheld, even though it was found to involve state action. In *Trustees of the University of Delaware v. Gebelein*, 420 A.2d 1191 (1980), the state's Court of Chancery found that the university's administration of a female-only scholarship program did constitute government action, subjecting the program to constitutional scrutiny. Applying the Fourteenth Amendment, the court upheld the fund, judging that its goal was not discriminatory, but rather *designed to address past discrimination.*

THE CONSTITUTIONAL LABYRINTH

When financial aid determinations involve "property" or "liberty" interests, *constitutional law* applies. A principal case in this area is *Corr v. Mattheis*, 407 F.Supp. 847 (1976). In *Corr*, several University of Rhode Island students took over the campus ROTC office. On top of disciplinary probation, the financial aid office used a federal statute prohibiting aid to those guilty of seizing property to justify mid-year termination of financial aid. The campus disciplinary proceedings had made no mention of any aid consequences.

The students sued, claiming a lack of due process. The court held that the students were indeed entitled to *notice and an opportunity to be heard* before termination of federal financial aid benefits. The court noted, however, that such due process may not be required for aid terminations for *academic* reasons.

In addition to due process, the constitutional principle of equal protection has great impact on financial aid programs. Of course, there is no constitutional guarantee of aid itself; but students applying for what aid is available must be treated in a uniformly fair manner.

Sex-based distinctions in public scholarships were severely limited by Title IX. In short, sex-based decision-making in financial aid awards was eliminated except when:

- the fund is established by a domestic or foreign will, trust, or gift;
- the fund is a study grant created by a foreign government;
- the fund is used for athletic scholarships; or
- the fund is provided to assist "personal appearance, poise, and talent" contest winners, even if the contest is limited to one sex.

Discrimination against *handicapped* persons is prohibited by Section 504 of the federal Rehabilitation Act. That law prohibits schools from providing less assistance to handicapped persons than to others, and also prohibits limitations on the amount of aid handicapped individuals can receive. As is the case with sex-based decision-making, funds from private wills and trusts that discriminate are kosher, so long as the *overall impact* of the total financial aid program is non-discriminatory.

Financial aid discrimination based on *age* is under the control of various statutes, including the Age Discrimination Act of 1975 and regulations for sundry federally sponsored aid programs. In general, age-based decision-making is unconstitutional, except for affirmative action.

Racial considerations in financial aid processes are more complex. A white Georgetown University law student challenged in court a financial aid formula granting 60% of the school's financial aid to its 11% minority population. The university defended the program as affirmative action. The court, finding that the white student received less aid than some minority students with less financial need, ruled that allocation of financial aid *explicitly based on race* is unconstitutional. Thus, Georgetown's financial aid program unlawfully discriminated on the basis of race. "While an affirmative action program may be appropriate to insure that all persons are afforded the same opportunities ... it is not permissible when it allocates scarce resources in favor of one race to the detriment of others," the federal court concluded. (*Flanagan v. President and Directors of Georgetown University*, 417 F.Supp. 377 (1976).)

While *Flanagan* ruled out race as an explicit factor in financial aid determinations, later decisions (such as the *Bakke* "reverse discrimination" case) support race as at least a *factor* in such decisions.

Financial discrimination against *non-state residents* by public higher education institutions, as in differential tuition plans, has met judicial favor in a variety of cases. For example, in *Vlandis v. Kline*, 412 U.S. 441 (1973), the U.S. Supreme Court recognized that "a state has a legitimate interest in protecting and preserving the quality of its colleges ... and the right of its own bona fide residents to attend such institutions on a preferential tuition basis." (Not all differential tuition plans or residency requirements have withstood court challenge, however.)

CONCLUSION

In addition to contractual, testamentary, and constitutional issues in financial aid, *state and federal legislation* is a major legal factor. State and federal regulation of financial aid, taken as a whole, is all-encompassing. Policies and guidelines attached to the ever-growing myriad of governmental financial aid programs are enormous legal factors in the consideration of any particular program.

Common-law principles, based on contractual, testamentary, constitutional, and legislative considerations, heavily regulate financial aid in higher education. In the case about tying the draft to aid receipt — the most recent test of the extent of governmental control and regulation of assistance programs — the government came out the winner. Eligibility for student financial aid can be conditioned on compliance with Selective Service laws. The U.S. Supreme Court agreed with the argument that this linkage is a reasonable means of improving that compliance.

While receipt of student financial aid is not constitutionally guaranteed, institutions cannot ignore basic fairness in making awards. Regulation of campus financial aid programs through contractual, testamentary, constitutional, and legislative means is designed to insure that basic fairness.

The College As Contractor

W hat is the nature of the relationship between students and colleges today?

For a long time, that relationship could be summed up with the words *in loco parentis* (in place of the parent). In recent decades, concern over constitutional rights and roles has put an end to that era. Today, the *contractual* nature of the relationship is well established. With the contract in place as both source and definor of rights and remedies, colleges and universities must be prepared to perform as agreed. If they do not, they will have to deal with the consequences: usually, a breach-of-contract lawsuit brought by students.

The courts, confronted with a greatly increased caseload in this area in recent years, have exercised caution in dealing with matters they perceive as strictly academic. When they have attacked the issue, they've been inconsistent. Courts in different jurisdictions have sometimes taken a narrow, sometimes a broad view of the student/institution relationship.

In the narrow view, courts have simply looked at printed materials — such as catalogs and regulations — to determine the specifics of the agreement that binds the parties. If it's in print, you're bound by it.

On the other hand, some courts have gone much further, examining an alleged contract by reviewing *all written and oral representations* that may contain implied terms. This interpretation allows the court to put itself into a student's shoes, to review what the student could or should have reasonably expected to occur as part of his arrangement with the school.

Student breach-of-contract suits can involve claims against almost any campus unit, but have generally been based on one of the following:

- failure to provide a promised academic program;
- poor courses;
- changed admission criteria;

- increased tuition; or
- class cancellations.

The existing case law in these areas can be instructive to both faculty and staff.

CHANGING HORSES

Failure to provide a program was at issue in *Lowenthal v. Vanderbilt University* (Tennessee, 1977). Midway through its initial management doctorate program, the university reevaluated the entire program and changed both the degree and evaluation requirements. Siding with angry students, the court ruled that the collapse of an academic program is indeed a breach of contract. The court held the school had violated its express promise to "provide a high quality of academic training." Tuition and expenses were awarded to the affected students, but their claims for book and travel expenses, and lost or diminished future earnings, were rejected.

Loss of accreditation was the beginning of trouble at the Ohio University School of Architecture in 1969. Faculty repeatedly reassured students that the program would continue. However, after several years, the school reevaluated the program and terminated it. Unhappy students sued, claiming the school had misrepresented its intentions and breached its contract with the students. In *Behrend v. State of Ohio*, 379 N.E.2d 617 (1977), the Ohio Court of Appeals found there was a contract:

"When a student enrolls in a college or university, pays his or her tuition and fees and attends such school, the resulting relationship may reasonably be constructed as being contractual in nature."

The court found that since the school had entered into a contract with its students, and was not able to comply with its terms, the contract was breached and damages were due to the injured parties.

Lowenthal reinforces the principle that program changes should be phased in with new students to avoid problems. Students have successfully sued to force schools to retain degree requirements and procedures existing at the time of their admissions. *Behrend* firmly establishes the nature of the student/school relationship as contractual, and suggests that once a contract is in place, significant breaches will lead to damages.

What if a student finds herself in a course that's just bad? Can she pursue a judicial solution? In an early test of "educational malpractice" in higher education, a Connecticut student did sue for that reason, claiming breach of contract because his course did not match the published description, and because he thought the content and presentation were poor. (He complained of few opportunities for discussion or evaluation.) The instructor and some classmates testified in opposition. The court, in *Ianniello v. University of Bridgeport*, ruled that, while a contract did exist, there had not been a significant breach. The court noted a reluctance to enter into a primarily academic dispute. In other words, how best to teach will be left to the teachers.

IT'S IN THE CATALOG

Catalog language bound the school in an admissions case, *Steinberg v. Chicago Medical School*, 371 N.E.2d 634 (1977). Claiming that criteria not found in the school's printed materials were used in admission evaluations, a rejected student responded with legal action. Ruling that the school was obligated to fulfill its promises, the court, based on contract theory, wrote that the student "was entitled to have his application judged according to the school's stated criteria."

Few things can create more campus unhappiness than *tuition increases*. At one time several years ago, some District of Columbia college students decided they were mad as hell, and not going to take it anymore. In *Basch v. George Washington University*, 370 A.2d 1364, they sued, claiming breach of contract because the school had raised its rates beyond estimations in its earlier publications. In dismissing the action, the court found that the published tuition projections had not established a contract for future tuition rates.

In another tuition challenge, students brought a class action against Northwestern Medical School in an effort to overturn "larger than reasonable" increases. The students maintained that tuition should go up only a reasonable amount during a term. They defined "reasonable" as the same level of rate increases occurring in previous years.

The court disagreed, finding that the student-school contract is renewed *each and every semester*. Thus, it is subject to change every semester. The court did not buy the argument that the school was taking advantage of the poor bargaining position of students midway through their educational programs.

Two early 1970s cases set down the legal principles for cases involving *cancellation of classes*. Both cases involved outright schedule changes due to campus unrest from anti-war demonstrations. In *Zumbrun v. University of Southern California*, 25 Cal.App.3d 1, an instructor cancelled classes halfway through the year and gave everyone a grade of B. One student sued, claiming breach of contract, and sought a return of tuition paid for the course (plus other damages). The court rejected a number of the student's claims, but did find that the student had not gotten what he had bargained for. In directing a lower court to assess damages, the court suggested the award in these circumstances should be minimal, at most a partial refund.

In viewing the student-school relationship as contractual, the courts have, in effect, established rights and responsibilities for both. To avoid breach-of-contract claims, schools should exercise care to *eliminate* any possible misunderstanding or misrepresentation, written and oral. In addition, campus policies should be clearly written — and followed. The language used should reserve the school's right to make program changes as necessary.

Remember, where the court finds a contract, the court will enforce a contract.

Principles

- In contract law, all outside materials — written and verbal — are deemed to be outside of the agreement, unless incorporated in the written contract.

- Most courts will try to reach a determination that a contract is valid and enforceable.

- The fair use doctrine of the Copyright Act permits copying and use of small portions of programs for teaching, research, and scholarship purposes.

- If a school-held record is "directly related to a student," the student may examine it, with some exceptions.

- After examining records, a student has the right to challenge the accuracy of any information included.

- If a student's challenge to the accuracy of recorded information reveals an error, the school must correct the record.

- Program changes should be phased in with new students to avoid problems.

- Campus policies should use language reserving the school's right to make program changes as necessary.

- While receipt of student financial aid is not constitutionally guaranteed, institutions cannot ignore basic fairness in making awards.

6. Student Groups and Activities

The College administration printed flyers notifying the sophomore class of the date and place of the picnic, and these flyers, containing drawings of beer mugs, were prominently displayed across the campus. Also, the internal regulations of the College prohibited the use of intoxicants by students under the age of twenty-one years. Thus the College, by its own regulations, recognized the inherent danger in the use of alcohol by immature students.
— *Bradshaw v. Rawlings*, 464 F.Supp. at 180-81 (1979)

In *Bradshaw*, a sophomore class "picnic" (drinking party) was capped by a serious car crash that left a student quadriplegic. The trial court had no trouble holding the school liable. Fortunately for Delaware Valley College (Pennsylvania), however, that decision was reversed on appeal by the Third Circuit U.S. Court of Appeals (612 F.2d 135 (1979).

But if one focuses only on the college's ultimate victory, it's easy to miss our main point, put this way in the trial court's opinion: "An educational institution may be held liable for negligence in its supervision of extracurricular activities."

Of course, whether "may" turns to "will" depends on many factors. And there are many possible settings for the asking and answering of that question. There's the student newspaper office; the fraternity house, or fraternity-sponsored activity; a host of other student organizations and their activities; the field trip or special event.

How Free Is the Campus Press?

Administrators continually walk a fine line between regulation and censorship of the campus press. The campus newspaper has all the duties and responsibilities of any campus organization, and the First Amendment's freedom-of-assembly and right-to-organize provisions apply to all campus clubs. However, there is no doubt that the First Amendment's relevance to the campus press goes beyond these all-purpose applications. How strongly does the principle of freedom of the press apply to the student newspapers? Is its application on campus different from what happens off campus?

The basic principle of freedom of the press on campus got a boost in *Joyner v. Whiting*, 477 F.2d 456 (1973). In that case, the college president cut off funding for the student newspaper in a dispute over articles about segregation. The court held the action violated the newspaper's constitutional rights, saying:

"It may well be that a college need not establish a campus newspaper, or if a paper has been established, the college may permanently discontinue publication for reasons wholly unrelated to the First Amendment. But if a college has a student newspaper, its publication cannot be suppressed because college officials dislike its editorial comment. Censorship of constitutionally protected expression cannot be imposed by suspending editors ... or asserting any other form of censorial oversight based on the institution's power of the purse."

In addition, *Joyner* looked at other methods colleges and universities sometimes use to control or eliminate campus publications — including suspension or termination of editors, reduction in circulation, elimination of controversial materials, and requirements for advance approval for controversial matters. The court's conclusion: "These methods cannot be employed when the purpose of them is to alter or block editorial content." The court saw some problems in the publication, but said termination of funding was an inappropriate way to resolve production difficulties.

PLAYING WITH THE FUNDING

In a more recent case, the state board of regents took a slightly different tack against the student paper at the Twin Cities campus of the University of Minnesota. In response to a "humor issue" (which many members of the campus and community evidently did not find humorous) the regents made student-fee funding for the paper voluntary, not mandatory. Students could get a refund of that portion of their fees at the paper's expense.

The newspaper challenged this change, contending the regents were retaliating for the humor issue. The editors claimed the new funding method was intended to restrict their press freedom by restricting their funding sources. In *Stanley v. Magrath*, 719 F.2d 279 (1983), a federal appeals court ruled that a public university may not base such actions on the paper's editorial content: "It is clear that the First Amendment prohibits the Regents from taking adverse action against the (paper) because the contents of the paper are occasionally blasphemous or vulgar."

To back up this decision, the court noted the testimony of several regents expressing displeasure with the paper, and saying their displeasure was in fact the reason for their support for the funding change. It also came out that funding methods for two less-controversial papers at other schools in the system went unchanged. It was clear that the paper's content motivated the Board's action, and action based on content alone is held to be unconstitutional.

A common response to dissatisfaction with campus newspapers is the firing of the editor. That method of control came under court scrutiny in *Schiff v. Williams*, 519 F.2d 257 (1975), a case out of Florida Atlantic University. The school's president fired the paper's editors, citing poor-quality work and lack of respect for school guidelines. The school argued that poor spelling and grammar reflected on the quality of the school.

The court sympathized with the embarrassment that a poor publication could cause, but said embarrassment is not a good enough reason to limit freedom of the press. "The right of free speech embodied in a student newspaper cannot be controlled except under special circumstances." The court found none.

As shown in *Joyner, Stanley,* and *Schiff*, public colleges and universities are extremely limited in the controls they can exercise over the student press. Various methods of control, including manipulation of key resources such as staff and funding, have been held unconstitutional when used by schools to direct, alter, or eliminate editorial content.

Of course, campus papers must adhere to the rules and regulations governing campus organizations generally, but administrators must be very careful any attempt to control or influence the student press does not stem from the paper's content or editorial opinion.

WHAT RIGHTS DO ADVERTISERS HAVE?

Is commercial speech, such as advertising, protected under the First Amendment? What controls, if any, is advertising in the campus press subject to? Careful review and application of known standards is the best protection from damage awards that college papers can get.

Only in recent years have the courts extended constitutional protection to advertising in general. A 1964 case, *New York Times Co. v. Sullivan*, 376 U.S. 254, helped define "editorial (issue-oriented) advertising." The U.S. Supreme Court ruled that an ad objecting to treatment of black citizens could not be rejected based on content. According to the court, the ad dealt with "matters of the highest public interest and concern," and thus deserved constitutional protection.

The high court expanded First Amendment protection of newspaper advertising content in 1975, ruling that an ad for a New York abortion service was protected in a Virginia publication, despite a Virginia statute making it illegal to "encourage or promote" abortions. The Court said that protected speech does not lose its protected status just because it appears in a commercial form. It found that the ad contained "factual material of a clear public interest" on an issue of public debate. *Bigelow v. Virginia*, 421 U.S. 809. (Advertising that is misleading, false, or deceptive is always subject to regulation, on and off campus.)

In general the courts have ruled that privately owned newspapers need not accept particular commercial or editorial advertising. *Chicago Joint Board v. Chicago Tribune Co.*, 435 F.2d 470 (1970). This principle translates to student newspapers at private schools, allowing them to closely control their content.

At public institutions, however, the courts have said that a campus newspaper that accepts any ads must accept editorial advertising. The test case here involved the University of Wisconsin-Whitewater in the late 1960s. The student paper staff had three times refused to print issue-oriented advertising on such matters as employee unions, discrimination, race relations, and the Vietnam War. The school enforced a faculty-staff committee rule against editorial advertising.

Students claimed the paper's refusal to print their ads was unlawful censorship, and sued. A federal court agreed, noting that student newspapers are important forums for the "dissemination of opinions and expression of opinion." Letters to the editor, the court found, are not an adequate outlet for editorial content.

The decision was upheld on appeal. "A state public body (university) which disseminates paid advertising of a commercial type may not reject other paid advertising on the basis that it is editorial in character," the appeals court wrote. The rule banning editorial ads was a university, not newspaper, policy. Thus it was a state action. *Lee v. Board of Regents of State Colleges*, 306 F.Supp. 1097.

(College editors can still review ads in advance and lawfully refuse them if they are obscene, libelous, or subversive. However, they can't refuse an ad simply because doing so would "protect the university from embarrassment." *Lee*.)

State involvement is a key element in judicial review of refused ads, as *Lee* demonstrates. However, courts take a different view of decisions by editors at public institutions not involving state action:

In *Mississippi Gay Alliance v. Goudelock*, 536 F.2d 1073, a homosexual interest group tried to place ads in the student newspaper at Mississippi State University. The editor refused to publish them. Student members of the Alliance sued, claiming a First Amendment violation. The court noted that the paper's faculty advisor, and the school administration, did not participate in the decision to refuse, and ruled the editor had the right "to accept or reject such material as he saw fit."

The appeals court agreed, on the ground that the action was not state-supported or sponsored. The higher court noted the paper was supported by student fees, and that the editor was elected by students, not the university. In addition, the court took note of the fact that state statutes prohibit homosexual contact, saying the editor has a right to keep the paper free from entanglement in illegal activities.

For college newspapers, advertising presents legal difficulties. However, such cases as *Lee* and *Mississippi Gay Alliance* provide basic guidelines for policy-making:

- Editorial advertising is considered constitutionally protected speech.

- Newspapers at private colleges are not bound by the First Amendment to the extent that they must accept all forms of advertising.

- If newspapers accept commercial advertising, they must then accept issue-oriented, or editorial, advertising.

- College newspapers do not have to publish advertising that is obscene, libelous, or incites unlawful actions.

- The extent of state control and influence determines whether refusal to run an ad is state-sponsored censorship. Students acting without administrative control or guidance can exercise editorial discretion.

Institutional Liability for Fraternities

The extent to which a university or fraternity can be held accountable for the consequences of not enforcing regulations was the issue in *Whitlock v. University of Denver*, 712 P.2d 1072. A fraternity member at the school received a $5.2 million judgment against the fraternity, the university, and the manufacturer and seller of a trampoline on which he was injured. The neck injury, which left the student quadriplegic, occurred on a trampoline owned by a campus fraternity recognized by the school. Prior to trial, settlements were reached out of court with all defendants except the university. During the trial, the following key points were made to the jury:

- The university had the power to cancel the fraternity's lease for "unlawful or dangerous conduct," but didn't.

- The presence of the trampoline was well-known to the university; it was on the front lawn of the house, and had been in and around the house for almost a decade.

- Several persons had been previously injured on the trampoline, and this, too, was known to campus officials.

- The lease established university maintenance responsibilities for the property and showed university control over the land and over such student organizations. For example, the school exercised controls over various fraternity activities, including greased-pole climbing and skateboarding.

- There is an inherent danger in the use of trampolines. The university gave evidence that the trampoline equipment it owned was kept in a secured room and could only be used under the supervision of a coach.

The jury determined the total amount of the injured student's damages as a result of the accident was $7.3 million. However, the jury found the student 28% responsible for his own injuries and, under comparative negligence laws, reduced the judgment to $5.2 million. The trial judge set aside the verdict on two grounds. He felt that the daily presence of the injured student in his wheelchair in court swayed the jury through "sympathy, passion, and prejudice." The judge also felt the student had been more negligent than the school.

The Colorado Court of Appeals found sufficient causes to reinstate the original jury verdict of $5.2 million. The appeals panel found that the university had a duty to exercise reasonable care to protect students, which it did not properly exercise, based on its control of fraternities, the prior injuries, the knowledge of the danger of trampolines, and its continued use on university property. The court determined that enough evidence was presented to support the jury decision and the trial judge should not have altered the findings. The court also found no cause to support the allegation that the presence of the injured party in the courtroom unduly influenced the jury's decision.

Finally, the Colorado Supreme Court threw out the damage award, ending the case in the university's favor. The court's conclusion: "There exists no special relationship between the parties that justifies placing a duty upon the University to protect (the plaintiff) from the well-known dangers of using a trampoline." Thus the state high court agreed with the trial-court judge's original opinion that, in essence, it was the injured student's own fault.

Although the university came out a winner in the end, we believe higher education administrators can take fair warning from the chronology of *Whitlock*. Not every court in the land is necessarily through with the *in loco parentis* doctrine. You may have to fight all the way to the state supreme court, or higher, to win a case like this. Thus, the best route is to prevent any such case from arising in the first place. The points made in the jury trial and enumerated above provide clues to the prudent, preventive route.

Generally, courts review higher education negligence suits by looking at a number of important factors:

- First, whether the action or inaction of the institution falls under the legal definition of a tort. The question first asked will be whether the school owed a duty to the injured person but failed to exercise due care to avoid the injury.

- Second, whether the school's actions are protected by an established defense recognized by the law that protects the institution from liability. Contributory negligence, in which the plaintiff's own fault offsets or negates liability, and assumption of risk, in which the plaintiff is judged to have accepted the risk of any consequences, are examples.

- Third, if there is a legal duty, what standard of care should be applied to the school. An earlier case, *Mortiboys v. St. Michael's College*, 478 F.2d 196 (1973), helped determine the standard of care owed by colleges to student plaintiffs. The court said the college must exercise "reasonable care under all circumstances." If the school is to be found liable, the dangerous condition would either have to be known to the school or have existed for a period long enough that the school should have known of the danger.

- Finally, before liability of the school is established, it must be shown that the action or inaction of the institution was the "proximate cause" of the injury and that there are in fact damages.

The $5.2 million award-that-almost-was in *Whitlock* dramatically demonstrates the extent to which some courts can and will hold colleges liable for activities of recognized student organizations.

Failure to follow rules or to enforce regulations can create serious liability problems. Also, failure to take adequate steps to correct dangers brought to institutional attention through previous incidents leads to liability risks. If a problem exists, correct it. There may not be a second chance — for the institution or for a student.

HAZING UNDER FIRE

The national trend toward greater college and university monitoring of fraternities' and sororities' activities, on and off campus, continues. The reason: high numbers of reported hazing incidents, substantial damage awards and settlements, and dramatic increases in liability insurance rates.

At Ohio State, trustees approved a measure extending campus jurisdiction of hazing violations to off-campus sites, such as band summer camps and fraternity and sorority houses. The action will allow the campus judicial office to discipline individuals or organizations involved in hazing.

Officials at both Oklahoma State and the University of Oklahoma have placed fraternities on probation for hazing incidents, acting against whole chapters even when only one or two members violated rules. The Oklahoma schools report a growing willingness of national fraternity offices to discipline chapters accused of hazing violations.

A University of Mississippi fraternity, under suspension for hazing, sponsored a campus appearance by the mother of a teenager killed in a New York hazing incident as a requirement to regain its charter. The program was videotaped for use at future meetings of the campus interfraternity council.

Escalating disciplinary actions show that schools *can* do something. A sorority at Wittenberg University (Ohio) was banned for at least three years after an injury to a pledge during a hazing incident. The chapter was ordered to vacate its campus house and prohibited from organizing on campus during that period.

The fallout was greater at North Carolina A&T State University after an incident in which several students complained they were hit over the head with two-by-four boards. School officials were ordered to testify in a criminal trial stemming from the incident. The university shortened the rush period, suspended the chapter for four years, and filed complaints against alleged participants.

In addition, state legislatures are getting involved. Half the states have anti-hazing laws, and that number will probably increase. In general, campus officials note these positive trends in controlling or eliminating hazing:

- Students today are more willing to report hazing incidents.

- Campus sanctions against whole chapters for violations by one or a few members have proven effective.

- National fraternity and sorority organizations have shown an increased willingness to sanction chapters.

What's a Liability Waiver Really Worth?

A midshipman at the U.S. Naval Academy was seriously injured when he landed on electric power lines during a parachute jump. He sued the firm which organized the jump for the school club. But the company, Parachutes Are Fun, Inc., said sorry, no damages. The reason? The midshipman had signed a release-of-liability form before the jump. In *Boucher v. Riner*, 514 A.2d 485 (1986), the court examined various types of releases, or waivers of liability. It was by no means the first case which questioned the effectiveness of tort liability releases used by colleges and universities.

A release is a document, signed by a person taking part in an event or activity, that indicates the program sponsors will not be held responsible in case of damage or injury. Most schools use these forms in the hope that the signed statement will protect them from liability. This hope springs from an assumption that the form "releases" the school from any obligations. Releases are common for field trips, athletic events, and potentially dangerous activities and instruction — like parachuting, or judo classes. But does the level of courts' acceptance of these forms match their widespread use?

THE WAIVER AS CONTRACT

Different courts, as usual, have interpreted releases and waivers differently. When deciding cases involving adults, some courts have accepted waivers where: (1) something of value (consideration) changed hands to make it contractually valid; (2) there is no evidence of fraud or duress; and (3) the language is very *specific* on the extent of the waiver.

For example, in *Popovich v. Empire Beauty Schools, Inc.*, 567 F.Supp. 1440 (1983), a federal court dealt with the case of the "permanent wave" that caused loss of hair, burns, and emotional distress. The customer claimed her injuries resulted from the school's negligence; but the school produced a signed waiver of liability. The form stated the school was protected from "any and all liability in any manner relating to services and treatment." The court ruled the release valid, finding it to be an enforceable contract. There was no showing of fraud, duress, accident or mistake; the language was clear, specific, and understood, in the court's view.

In a case in a resort setting, a guest injured in a fall from a rented bicycle sued for damages, contending the facility failed to properly inspect and maintain the bikes. The resort responded with a signed release, showing the guest had agreed to "indemnify and hold [the resort] free and harmless" of responsibility for the bike and its operation. The court found the language clear, and granted summary judgment to the resort. (*Gimpel v. Host Enterprises, Inc.*, 640 F.Supp. 972 (1986).)

As the beauty school and bike cases illustrate, some jurisdictions do uphold exculpatory clauses. They view releases as contracts, look for the elements that make for good, enforceable contracts, and take the position that adults can contract away their right to sue others for negligence.

PUBLIC POLICY AND WAIVERS

On the other side, there is considerable case law involving college and university release forms that have met with judicial disapproval. Courts which reject liability waivers generally do so on the basis of *public policy*. They claim (and in some states, are backed up by legislation) that releases for future negligent acts could cause failure to take proper precautions, contributing to injuries and damage. In addition, courts are very hesitant to allow individuals or organizations to "bargain away" their legal rights to sue or be sued. Campus-based cases involving parachuting, dental schools, and hockey clinics support the public-policy argument.

In *Gross v. Sweet*, 407 N.Y.S. 2d 254 (1978), a student at a parachuting school broke his leg on his first jump. Before the jump, he had signed a "responsibility form" accepting responsibility for the jump. The court concluded the form did *not* serve as a complete block of legal action against the school; the suit was allowed to continue on grounds other than responsibility for the jump, including faulty instruction and alleged failure to follow federally mandated procedures. The relationship between student and teacher was of special concern to the court; it found the release could not bar action for faulty instruction, as a matter of public policy.

In another case involving "responsibility forms," the parents of a student injured during a Bowdoin College hockey clinic sued, claiming the school was negligent in its conduct of the clinic. A jury awarded the student-player $50,000 in damages. On appeal, the school argued the responsibility statements signed by the parents should shield the school from liability. In *Doyle v. Bowdoin College*, 403 A.2d 1206 (1979), the court rejected that argument, ruling the forms weren't true releases or waivers. Therefore, the school couldn't use the forms to deny responsibility for its own negligence.

What happens when a dental student breaks a patient's jaw during negligent treatment? Is the outcome different if the patient signed a release? In *Emory University v. Porubiansky*, 282 S.E.2d 903 (1981), the injured patient sued, but the school replied there could be no damages because of a signed "information-consent" form. The Georgia Supreme Court disagreed, noting that those practicing a profession are expected to exercise a reasonable degree of skill and care — and ruling they should not be allowed to violate those standards through a contractual arrangement. *No written contract can exempt professionals from their standards of care.*

FREE CHOICE A MUST

The *circumstances* and *language* of release forms are important factors in their validity (or lack of it). Some court decisions stress that the parties to the contract must have bargained on equal footing, freely consenting to the agreement, for it to have effect. Also, courts tend to look hard at the language in releases, to make sure it was clear and direct. Without explicit language, courts can find that there was no agreement on the terms of the release, invalidating it. For instance, if a form is meant to protect an institution from liability due to negligence, the word *negligence* had better appear on the form. Campus cases involving field trips and dental work highlight these areas of judicial concern.

The circumstances surrounding a release came under scrutiny in *Whittington v. Sowela Technical Institute*, 438 So.2d 236 (1983). Nursing students were asked to sign a release form for a "voluntary" field trip to a hospital. Participating students received double credit hours, but no alternative class was offered for those not participating. The overcrowded van used for the trip (driven by a student) was involved in an accident; the husband of a student killed in the accident sued.

The court, despite the presence of signed release forms, found that the circumstances indicated the deceased student had not given "free and deliberate consent." Thus, the release forms were invalid. Public policy considerations were also a factor in the case.

The importance of "clear and unambiguous" language in liability releases is obvious from *Abramowitz v. NYU Dental Center*, 494 N.Y.S. 2d 721 (1985). A clinic patient undergoing treatment was asked to sign a form containing several sections of biographical data and financial information. At the bottom, in an untitled section in smaller type, was waiver-of-liability language.

After a lower state court had extensively reviewed the form, an appellate panel ruled that its language was ambiguous as to whether liability for negligence was being waived, because the word *negligence* never appeared. Citing the time when the clinic presented it for consideration; the position and type size of the waiver section; and the ambiguous language, the court ruled that the form did not release the clinic from liability for its acts of negligence.

In short, the language and circumstances of a release must reveal a clear understanding between the parties which precisely defines the liability that is being waived.

CONCLUSION

In *Boucher*, the case involving the injured U.S. Naval Academy parachutist, the court reviewed state statutes, the language and circumstances of the waiver. It ruled that Maryland does not have a public policy preventing parties from waiving liability in advance. Therefore, the midshipman had the right to freely waive any and all rights to sue for injuries due to negligence. The court upheld the waiver, eliminating any possibility of recovering damages.

Where do these differing opinions in different states leave colleges and universities regarding release forms?

These forms are still very useful, and in some circumstances, very effective. First, they serve to warn participants in advance of potential dangers; thus, after the fact, they show that those participants may have voluntarily assumed the risks that later resulted in injuries. Second, injured persons may refrain from bringing suit because of signed release forms. In addition, release forms can be a public-relations device for schools, allowing them to demonstrate that there was adequate warning of danger. Finally, in some jurisdictions, a good release form will in fact release one party from liability to the other. In all these ways, liability waivers serve higher education, and justify their continued use.

A Fresh Look at
Student Group-College Relations

Are they "of" or "at"? It's a simple question, with a complex answer, when you're talking about the relationship between student organizations and colleges. Of particular concern is the growing fear of institutional liability for fraternities' and sororities' negligence.

A jury found a fraternity member 7% negligent and his college 93% at fault for a hazing incident. Although the judgment was ultimately overturned, cases like this have forced a reexamination of these relationships.

MAKE A STATEMENT

A predictable outcome of this reexamination has been a dramatic surge in use of written relationship statements.

Relationship statements define the partnership between organization and school, enumerating the rights and responsibilities of both. For a college, such statements should serve several purposes — clarifying what recognition means to the group, establishing campus standards, and answering the question of liability. From a student organization point of view, the statement defines the relationship between organization and school, preserving as much independence in internal affairs as possible.

Good relationship statements serve these purposes, and more. They take into consideration the school's needs and the student organization's wants, and strike an appropriate balance between the two. And they should be drafted to last, dealing not only with current conditions, but with the future. Good relationship statements are negotiated, not decreed. And they have a mechanism to insure accountability, to identify and resolve problems before they become too serious and threaten the relationship.

The legal implications of recognition become important when developing a sound relationship statement. In turn, the type of higher education institution involved — public or private — is an important consideration when examining the legal limits on recognition, discipline, and discrimination:

At state universities and colleges, student organizations have a *constitutional right to exist*. The U.S. Supreme Court upheld the First Amendment's guarantees of assembly and association for these groups when it overturned the denial of recognition to a campus Students for a Democratic Society (SDS) chapter in *Healy v. James*, 408 U.S. 169 (1972). Private schools have far greater latitude in deciding what organizations are recognized, although the recent dispute over a gay student organization at Georgetown University may signal a change in this.

Once recognized, organizations may be subject to discipline, and a good relationship statement should deal with this area. At a public school, an organization member is entitled to constitutional due process rights anytime her property or liberty interests are affected. Private institutions are required to be fair, but only in accordance with published policies and procedures. However, once those rules are published, they form a binding contract. A private school cannot change the rules just because the administration changes its mind.

IN IT, BUT NOT OF IT

Bringing discipline into relationship statements with Greek-letter organizations is complicated by their legal status. National fraternities are generally corporations, incorporated in their state of origin. The local chapter is an unincorporated association, although a house may be owned or leased by a housing corporation, incorporated in the state where the house is located. What all this means is that you must fully understand the nature of the organizations before you establish a discipline process. For example, an organization's charter is granted by the corporate national, and no campus action can lift it. While the *existence* of the chapter depends on the national, the *recognition* of the chapter or the granting of certain *rights* may fully depend on the school.

At the heart of the issue of relationships between fraternal organizations and colleges is the "of" or "at" question, first considered at length several years ago at Michigan State University. In a 1982 incident, the president refused to intercede after a fraternity dismissed a homosexual member. The president chose not to apply campus anti-discrimination policies to the group, saying the fraternity had a special relationship to the school, but was *not part of* the school.

The University of Virginia has taken the "not part of the school" principle one step further: Instead of developing relationship statements, Virginia creates "Contracted Independent Organizations." The idea is to limit the school's exposure to liability from student organizations by specifically defining the limits of university authority. While the school recognizes the value of cultural, recreational, and social student organizations, UV wants it clearly understood by all that the organizations are "not part of or controlled by the university." The school takes the position that it is not responsible for the acts of student organizations, period.

Thus, the University of Virginia has rejected altogether the concept of recognition, and has rejected relationship statements along with it. Student organizations can operate on campus, with or without campus benefits. The university is a public corporation, and declares the Contracted Independent Organizations (CIOs) to be not part of that corporation. Accordingly, its agreement with student organizations says, "The CIO is not an agent, servant, or employee of the university, but rather is an independent contractor which manages its own affairs." Organizations under this arrangement may use the name of the school by indicating the club is "at," not "of" UV. The agreement specifically limits use of the university name to this language.

Of course, if only the school and the organization understood this "contracted independent" status, the contract would not fully serve the intended purpose of limiting liability. Therefore, the school requires student groups to explain that they are part of the university community, but not part of the university itself, in their letters, contracts, and publications.

In exchange for signing the agreement, stating the institution is not liable for organizational acts and omissions, groups have access to campus space and services.

CONCLUSION

There is a relationship of some kind between colleges and student organizations, and the extent to which institutions can transfer liability away from themselves through use of written contracts is unclear at this time. However, what the University of Virginia and schools developing written relationship statements are doing is focusing attention on an important issue.

By defining student organization-school relationships; developing the terms, expectations, and conditions of the relationship; and examining specific needs and concerns, colleges can best balance the interests of the campus and student organizations. Are your organizations "of" or "at"? It can make a big difference.

Principles

- Various methods of control, including manipulation of key resources such as staff and funding, have been held unconstitutional when used by schools to direct, alter, or eliminate editorial content of student newspapers.

- If newspapers accept commercial advertising, they must then accept issue-oriented, or editorial, advertising.

- Failure to take adequate steps to correct dangers brought to institutional attention through previous incidents leads to liability risks.

- The importance of clear and unambiguous language in liability releases is obvious.

- Good written relationship statements for student organizations have a mechanism to insure accountability, to identify and resolve problems before they become too serious and threaten the relationship.

7. Faculty and Staff

Perhaps surprising, but by now well documented, the relative representation and status of women as faculty members at universities and colleges deteriorated from the 1930s to 1970. The proportion of women serving in academic positions declined. Salary differentials associated with sex were marked and prevailed for every race. Legislation in the 1960s prohibiting sex discrimination in employment left academic employment untouched. The Equal Pay Act did not apply to academic and professional employees until amended in July 1972. Title VII excluded academic employment until its scope was enlarged by the Equal Employment Opportunity Act of 1972. State fair employment practice laws, even when they covered campus hiring and promotions, remained untried in this area.

  — *Kunda v. Muhlenberg College*, 621 F.2d at 550-51 (1980), quoting *Sex-Based Discrimination*, by Davidson, Ginsburg, and Kay (1974)

The feminist movement was indeed a late arrival on the college campus, which along with the world of rock 'n roll was one of the last bastions of male chauvinism. The pendulum has swung since the federal anti-discrimination laws were brought to bear on higher education.

But sex discrimination in hiring and tenure is only one area of education employment law the courts have gingerly stepped into since the early '70s. There are also the matters of sexual harassment; employment reference checks, and the questions of privacy and defamation they raise; movements toward collective bargaining by faculty (nowhere does the contrast between public and private institutions show up in sharper relief); equal pay for equal work; and employees' own free speech in this very First Amendment-oriented setting.

Sexual Harassment: Campus Powder Keg

In and out of the classroom, students are vulnerable to sexual harassment. In the past decade, growing numbers of faculty have been fired or suspended because of it. An associate professor at San Jose State University was dismissed after being accused by students of fondling, embracing, and propositioning them. A Santa Monica Community College physics instructor was accused of sexual harassment four times; the fifth time, he lost his job on evidence provided by complaining students. The list goes on. Thirty-one percent of those responding to a 1986 University of Missouri survey complained of receiving sexual advances from faculty members.

What exactly *is* sexual harassment? Let's start with the Equal Employment Opportunity Commission's definition, from its Guidelines on Sex Discrimination:

"Unwelcome sexual advances, requests for sexual favors, and other verbal or physical conduct of a sexual nature ... when

(1) submission to such conduct is made either explicitly or implicitly a term or condition of an individual's employment

(2) submission to or rejection of such conduct by an individual is used as the basis for employment affecting such individual, or

(3) such conduct has the purpose or effect of unreasonably interfering with an individual's work performance or creating an intimidating, hostile or offensive working environment."

As we shall see, governmental and legal definitions do not tell the whole story. But they are a starting point.

The problem of sexual harassment on college campuses has *surfaced* in the past decade, although it was probably there for many, many years before that. The big difference in recent years is the attention and response given to the problem. Congress and the state legislatures have enacted laws to protect individuals from sexual harassment, and the courts have backed these civil rights laws. Title IX of the Educational Amendments of 1972 prohibits sexual discrimination in education programs and activities receiving federal assistance; Title VII of the Civil Rights Act of 1964 has been held to protect employees at independent institutions from harassment. The U.S. Supreme Court, in the 1986 case of *Meritor Savings Bank v. Vinson*, 106 S.Ct. 2399, adopted the EEOC definition of sexual harassment as a national legal standard.

Given that sexual harassment of students and staff is a real problem — from a personal *and* legal perspective — college and university administrators must fully understand the issue; have appropriate policies in place to deal with it; take necessary steps to inform campus populations of the policies; and enforce the policies. To avoid damages (personal and monetary), the best course is through *understanding*, *planning*, and *education*.

TOWARD BETTER UNDERSTANDING

Meritor involved a bank teller's claims of harassment by a supervisor. Sexual advances were made, and the advances were not welcome. Importantly, the advances were made to appear as conditions of employment. Finally, those activities reached a point of visibility such that any employer should have been aware of them.

By endorsing the EEOC definition of harassment, the Court established some legal standards for harassment claims. Even more important to higher education administrators, colleges and universities in their role as employers can be held responsible for damages due to sexual harassment when the conditions in *Meritor* are met. Those conditions are (1) when the employer knows or should know of the offender's behavior, *or* (2) when the harassing employee has the power to hire or fire the harassed employee. The case reaffirmed the principle that employers are responsible for sexual harassment by supervisors, a principle dating back to the '70s (*Barnes v. Costle*, 561 F.2d 983 (1977); *Tomkins v. Public Service Electric and Gas Co.*, 568 F.2d 1044 (1977); and *Munford v. Barnes and Co.*, 441 F.Supp. 459 (1977)).

In addition to the EEOC guidelines approved in *Meritor*, the National Advisory Council on Women's Educational Programs has a definition of *classroom* harassment:

"... harassment in which the faculty member covertly or overtly uses the power inherent in the status of a professor to threaten, coerce, or intimidate a student to accept sexual advances or risk reprisal in terms of a grade, a recommendation, or even a job."

The law, whether legislative or judge-made, cannot fully define sexual harassment. It can provide a framework for examining claims, but it cannot produce a comprehensive list of do's and don'ts. Evaluation of any given campus circumstance involving claims of harassment depends partly on established standards, partly on a "reasonable person" test. That is, would a reasonable person find the alleged behavior offensive? Common sense, along with the legal framework, determines the standards from which campuses should draw their policies and actions.

Higher education sexual harassment cases are among the most difficult to deal with. In many cases, it comes down to deciding who to believe. An allegation is made; a denial is made. What's left can be very damaging to everybody, unless handled properly.

A grades-for-sexual-involvement case in Indiana illustrates the strict standards often applied to educators in sexual harassment cases. A Ball State University music instructor lost his job over allegations of sexual misconduct, and appealed to the courts for help. Instead, he and others similarly situated got some advice: The Seventh Circuit U.S. Court of Appeals held that a professor's "conduct is not to be viewed in the same context as would conduct of an ordinary person on the street. Rather, it must be judged in the context of the relationship existing between a professor and his students within an academic environment. University professors occupy an important place in our society and have concomitant ethical obligations." (*Korf v. Ball State University*, 726 F.2d 1222 (1984).)

A PLAN OF ACTION

Be prepared for sexual harassment allegations: Have a plan in place. If the Boy Scouts' principle is not enough incentive, consider Title IX of the Educational Amendments of 1972, which requires the development of written and well-publicized policies defining and prohibiting sexual harassment, as well as a system of resolving complaints with "appropriate due process."

Any campus system of dealing with allegations of harassment must be *swift* and *effective*. In addition, the process has to both *be* fair and *appear* to be fair to the accusing and to the accused. Finally, *confidentiality* should be preserved to the extent possible, to insure that (1) complainants feel comfortable coming forward, and (2) those falsely accused are not tainted unnecessarily.

What constitutes "due process" for staff members accused of sexual harassment may be more contractual than constitutional. However, make sure your system includes the following basic elements, to insure fairness:

- A *signed complaint* must be the starting point, and must be shared with the accused. After that, conclude an investigation and hearing expediently.

- Maintain as much confidentiality as possible; give the parties an opportunity to provide all relevant materials, and to respond to materials presented by the other party.

- Make a record of the evidence and hearing; see to it that the hearing decision is based only on the record as established.

EDUCATING THE MASSES

Even though education is the obvious purpose of a higher education institution, often the residents of campuses are less than fully informed about institutional policies. In the case of sexual harassment policies, the importance of getting the word out cannot be overemphasized. Establishment of a policy and grievance process is not enough; take steps to fully educate students, faculty, and staff on *what* sexual harassment is, what the potential *damages* are, and *where* to go if they think it has occurred.

The education stage is really a part of the planning stage; the two go together. In fact, a sexual harassment education program is the best plan a campus can have to fight harassment and protect itself from litigation. Looked at this way, development and implementation of policies and processes called for under Title IX is an important part of the education program.

The action a campus administration takes in regard to sexual harassment depends in part on the school, but is in part dictated by societal concern. At the same time a third of the students at the University of Missouri claimed to have been sexually harassed, 49% of non-tenured female faculty at Harvard University reported at least one instance of sexual harassment by a superior! A federal government survey of its work force estimated that employee turnover, sick leave, and lost productivity due to sexual harassment cost the government $287 million between 1985 and 1987 alone.

Sexual harassment may be difficult to define and difficult to prosecute, but it cannot be ignored. The damage and potential damage — on a personal and institutional scale — demands attention and action on campus today.

Getting and Giving Information About Employees

The threat of invasion-of-privacy or defamation lawsuits has made it more difficult for colleges and universities to give out information on current or past employees, and more difficult to ask for information on prospective employees. Fear of litigation over references and recommendations is causing a reevaluation of colleges' role in the employment process. The large number of discrimination claims based on employment decisions makes it more important than ever for schools to handle references and reference checks carefully.

Private-sector employers tend to centralize and control hiring information through a personnel operation. That way, they hope to minimize legal risks. But higher education hiring doesn't always lend itself to this approach, since many individual departments and other units handle employment screening. The decentralized approach to hiring makes it extremely important for search-committee members to understand the legal limitations on reference checks.

GETTING THE LOWDOWN

The key rule to remember for reference checks is this: Items which you cannot directly ask of a candidate, you can't legally ask of references. That restricts questioning to matters *directly related to job performance.* If you ask an unlawful question, but don't use the reply in your hiring decision, the assumption will still be that the unlawful question was a significant factor in that decision.

Treat all information obtained through reference checks as confidential, with access limited to those with a role in the hiring process. If reference materials find their way into hands beyond those with a need to know, it could be seen as an invasion of the candidate's privacy.

Universities often use a system of spot-checking references. If you're going to spot-check, make the rules consistent. Check out references on the same basis (for example, one out of three) for all candidates. This helps insure that there is no opportunity for discriminatory practices to develop.

Whatever system of reference checks you use, remember that terminating an employee is much harder than not hiring someone in the first place. References are a key element in avoiding bad hires. Use them wisely.

Search panels should use a consistent format for reference checks to avoid legal difficulties. Among the acceptable reference questions:

- How long did the employee work there?
- How well did she perform?
- What tasks and skills were involved?

- At what level of responsibility?
- Was job performance up to standards?
- Why did the employee leave?
- Was she effective in dealing with peers, superiors, and students?

Don't inquire into periods of unemployment that fall before or after the job reference you are checking. Experts suggest this could lead to charges of refusal to hire on the basis of involuntary unemployment, which in turn could be construed as discrimination against minorities. You can ask questions about potential, if the applicant is a candidate for a position that requires greater skill than her last job. You may ask past employers about disciplinary problems, if you ask the same question in all reference checks for the position.

As you might expect, there also is a list of key questions *not* to ask of candidates. For instance:

- Has the employee ever filed or threatened to file discrimination charges?
- Has she had difficulties with marriage, credit, age, or physical or mental problems?
- How will she find child care?
- Will her spouse approve of what she is doing?
- What political or religious preferences does the employee have?

All the questions you should avoid in candidate interviews are also off limits for reference checks. Inquiries into the wrong areas leave a school open to serious affirmative action/equal opportunity charges. Also on the "no" list: sharing information you already have with people you are checking out references with. Verify dates of previous employment, and similar data, by *asking the same questions*, not sharing the answers you already have. Violations of a candidate's privacy rights can have dire legal consequences.

GIVING THE LOWDOWN

Is it safer to receive, or give reference information? If you do it correctly, it makes no difference. When asked to give references or recommendations for past employees, the key is accuracy. *If you provide accurate information, you and your school will be protected —* it's that simple.

What topics should you cover when giving a reference? *Only job performance by the employee*, nothing else. Charges of discrimination or defamation spring mainly from the fertile field of information not related to job performance, or from inaccurate information.

A former employee's punctuality, attendance, quantity and quality of work, and an evaluation of potential based on past performance are all acceptable responses. Always depend on facts for responses; make no guesses. Stay away from comments about age, physical or mental disabilities, or periods of unemployment. Do not offer information about previous discrimination complaints, to prevent charges of campus retaliation for past incidents.

It is true that negative information about candidates, even if accurate, can draw charges of defamation (that is, slander or libel) by disgruntled job-seekers. For this reason, some employers limit their responses to dates of employment. That may serve an immediate purpose, but society is poorly served in the long run if employers feel unable to share proper information on job applicants. The best course of action is not to *volunteer* negative information, but give it if requested. Be helpful — and legally safe — by providing references that are accurate and limited to job performance.

One way to add some protection against possible defamation or invasion-of-privacy charges is to use *release forms*. A release or consent form can help identify the type and extent of materials to be released, thus preventing misunderstandings with ex-employees.

Ask the purpose of any request for information before giving out information. Not only prospective employers, but insurance companies, credit record firms, and others often seek personal information from former employers. Beware an invasion of privacy with such inquiries. Ask to see a consent form, and ask for the questions in writing.

Colleges and universities are major employers today. Every day, those employed in higher education look for jobs in the private sector, private-sector employees seek college jobs, and college employees move on to other institutions. Only through a well-thought-out plan of giving, and asking for, references, can employees' and employers' interests be served — legally and well.

Faculty Collective Bargaining: A Private vs. Public Affair

Boston University faculty members do not have a right to collective bargaining. That's the ruling handed down by a federal appeals court after 12 years of litigation about the role of faculty members at private colleges. The dispute dates to the mid-'70s, when a faculty union formed at the school and the school refused to bargain with it. The decision — so long in coming — raises fundamental questions about the status of faculty at private and public institutions.

YESHIVA AND BEYOND

The First U.S. Circuit Court of Appeals upheld a 1986 National Labor Relations Board (NLRB) ruling in making the Boston University decision. Both decisions were based on an earlier test of the same issue in *NLRB v. Yeshiva University*, 444 U.S. 672 (1980). In *Yeshiva*, the U.S. Supreme Court overturned years of campus collective-bargaining rulings in one stroke by declaring that private-school faculty at many schools could not participate in collective bargaining because they were part of management.

The ruling in *Boston University Chapter, American Association of University Professors v. NLRB* averred that BU faculty could not collectively bargain under the National Labor Relations Act (NLRA) because they had authority over academic matters and had an important role in campus governance. The court rejected the faculty's arguments that they have little impact on management of the university and should be protected by federal statute.

The nation's high court laid down the law in *Yeshiva* as follows: At institutions where faculty have control of the academic process and participate in campus hiring, tenure, promotion, and some financial processes, they have management status, and cannot organize under the law for purposes of collective bargaining. The divided (5-4) opinion did acknowledge that some faculty members at some institutions may not be part of management, but offered no test — producing a situation in which determinations of status are made on a case-by-case basis.

WHO MANAGES?

The fairly clean distinction between labor and management in American industrial settings does not translate to campus. The principle behind the NLRA's exclusion of management from collective bargaining is that employees who exercise authority on behalf of the employer cannot be expected to divide their loyalties between the employer and a union.

From that basis, litigation has focused on *which* employees are management, and which aren't. Reviewing this in *Yeshiva*, the Court said that the faculty at a private college control the "product to be produced, the terms upon which it will be offered, and the customers who will be served," and so faculty constitute management. Faculty control of or decision-making in curriculum, scheduling, teaching assignments, admissions, grades, hiring, tenure and promotion all contributed to the Court's finding.

The NLRB, which had ruled in favor of Yeshiva faculty's collective bargaining in that case, argued that faculty involvement in such issues was limited to application of professional expertise, and that faculty members' participation was on behalf of the faculty itself, not the institution. But the court majority disagreed, commenting that the faculty's professional interests could not be separated from those of the institution, and thus faculty would be treated as management to avoid "divided loyalty" problems.

THE PUBLIC EYE

Yeshiva and related decisions focus on private colleges and universities. What about public institutions? Clearly, there are two distinct sets of rules for campus collective bargaining, depending on the "private" or "public" nature of the institution. While the NLRB has asserted jurisdiction over private schools and their faculty for two decades, public post-secondary education is exempt from federal labor relations laws, and subject only to state authority.

A majority of states have passed legislation that permits full or limited collective bargaining by state college employees. The degree of unionization and bargaining permitted varies from state to state, from full organizing rights, to an opportunity to "meet and confer" with officials, to no rights at all.

The exemption of public post-secondary education itself has prompted litigation challenging accepted definitions of "public" and "private." The University of Vermont, which receives a substantial direct subsidy from the state, was found by the NLRB in 1976 to be "private." The Board ruled that because the state chartered the school as a private non-profit institution and did not govern it as a political unit of the state, the school's employees were protected under federal labor laws.

STANDARDS

In the wake of *Yeshiva*, the NLRB drafted guidelines for future determinations of faculty managerial status. The *degree of faculty authority in governance* is a key factor here. The NLRB looks at faculty authority over:

- courses to be taught
- when courses are to be offered
- development of teaching standards and grading policies
- admissions and graduating decisions
- size of student body, tuition and fees charged, and site of the school
- teaching loads, absence policies, and enrollment levels
- hiring, salaries, tenure, leaves, terminations and promotions.

Another factor for NLRB review in faculty-managerial disputes is the *degree to which faculty interests differ from institutional interests.* If they are seen as identical (as was the case in *Yeshiva*), collective bargaining creates divided loyalties. If faculty interests are different from those of the institution, that problem may be avoided — although the *Yeshiva* court left little room for such a decision.

A third factor established by the Board in faculty review is *accountability.* Here again, the *Yeshiva* court did not view this as significant. The Court saw accountability as important for employees outside of education only, but the NLRB included the factor in its guidelines anyway.

Finally, the NLRB named *amount of time faculty members spend on managerial-type duties*. This commercial or industrial test for classifying employees was imported to campus by the NLRB, although *Yeshiva* focused only on the *nature* of the duties.

Using the principles developed by the Supreme Court in *Yeshiva*, and the Board's own later rulings, the NLRB found in 1986 that the faculty role at Boston University was predominant in the school's principal business — providing education and research. BU faculty members, the Board ruled, were therefore managerial. The U.S. Court of Appeals has now upheld that decision. Faculty representatives at BU disagree with the ruling, and have asked for a rehearing, contending they lack the level of influence over academic matters demanded by the *Yeshiva* test.

Similar NLRB decisions against private-school faculty unionization have ended organizing efforts under the NLRA at Fairleigh Dickinson University in New Jersey and North Carolina's Livingstone College.

Yeshiva remains the basic test for determining faculty status at private colleges and universities, and strong faculty involvement in decision-making has led to more pegging of faculty members as managers. Faculties that are managerial under these standards *do* have a constitutional right to organize; but don't have the protection of the NLRA and other federal labor relations laws. In other words, they don't have the legal leverage to make schools bargain with them in good faith about employment issues.

Equal Pay for Equal Work Comes to Campus

"Employees doing equal work should be paid equal wages, regardless of sex." That language in the federal Equal Pay Act is over 25 years old, but only in the last decade or so has the issue taken root on college and university campuses. In fact, before 1972, most faculty positions weren't covered by the Act; they fell under an exemption for "professional, executive, and administrative" employees. Claims of sex discrimination in higher education led to removal of that exemption.

Georgia Southwestern College's faculty salary system was investigated by the U.S. Dept. of Labor in recent years. The review found at least six instances in which the college paid female faculty members less than their male counterparts in other disciplines. Finding no apparent justification for the salary differences, the department sued the school for non-compliance with the Equal Pay Act. To aid our understanding of this case, let's briefly review the Act itself and its implications on campus:

NEUTRALITY: THE BEST POLICY

Both the Equal Pay Act and the Civil Rights Act of 1964 (Title VII) prohibit discrimination in employment on the basis of sex. However, the Equal Pay Act offers the clearest language on the issue: It mandates that men and women be paid equally "for equal work on jobs the performance of which requires equal skill, effort, and responsibility," and which have similar working conditions. To make a case under the Act, a complaining employee must show that pay is unequal under these conditions. If she establishes that much, the burden of proof moves to the college to show that there is an acceptable, non-sex-related basis for the pay differential. There are four exceptions to the equal-pay requirement found in the Act:

- a seniority system
- a merit system
- salary systems that measure quality or quantity
- other sex-neutral factors

There are legitimate reasons for many pay differentials, of course. A court faced with an equal-pay dispute looks at what caused the difference: sex-based discrimination, or acceptable exemptions to the law.

Note that the list of exemptions provides a clue to the best course of action, which can be summed up: Be prepared. If there are pay differences between the sexes at your institution, know the reason. Not having a reason (even if there is no conscious effort to discriminate) may mean losing an equal-pay lawsuit, if the plaintiff gets past the *prima facie* elements of unequal pay, equal work, and similar conditions. The Rhode Island School of Design lost an equal-pay case due to its haphazard approach to salary administration (*Melanson v. Rantoul*, 536 F.Supp. 271 (1982)).

Neutral factors which legally contribute to sexual pay differentials include prior experience, degrees earned, sources of degrees, and publishing records. Even competitive market factors can legally affect campus salary structures. Courts in complex salary cases have tried to steer a middle ground between excessive intrusion into campus affairs and tolerance for illegal behavior.

There are two basic methods campus-based litigants have successfully used to prove pay inequities in court. A simple averaging of male and female salaries on campus is *not* one of them. Courts require more specific proof of sex-based pay disparity.

The most commonly adopted method of proof is called "pairing." This involves a faculty member's comparing her job to another specific job on campus, in an attempt to show that equal work is being performed for unequal pay. The pairing method was first successful in *Hein v. Oregon College of Education*, 178 F.2d 910 (1983).

The other method of proving sex-based pay inequities is statistical, using multiple regression analysis. This technique assesses a variety of variables as they relate to pay rates, attempting to show that sex-related bias is the key factor in differences. Statistical evidence is most common in class action equal-pay cases. *Dothard v. Rawlinson*, 433 U.S. 321 (1977), is an example.

AFFIRMATIVE REACTION

The Equal Pay Act was designed to address wage and salary discrimination against women. "It sought to overcome the age-old belief in women's inferiority and to eliminate the depressing effects on living standards of reduced wages for female workers and the economic and social consequences which flow from it." (*Shultz v. Wheaton Glass Co.*, 1970.) However, as institutions have sought to cure past inequities on behalf of female workers, the other side of the coin has turned up. Several male challenges to equal-pay efforts on campus have hit the docket in recent years.

In *Ende v. Board of Regents of Northern Illinois University*, 32 Empl. Prac. Dec. P33, 932 (1983), male faculty members sued the school for adjusting female salaries, but not theirs. The court sided with the university, citing voluntary affirmative action cases such as *University of California Regents v. Bakke*, 98 S.Ct. 2733 (1978): "While this court is sympathetic to the plight of the (male employees), it is clear that the (school) was making a reasonable, good faith effort to adjust inequities which admittedly had existed for many years."

However, other courts take a different view: In *Lyon v. Temple University*, 543 F.Supp.

1372 (1982), male employees sued when female faculty salaries were raised. The court overturned the university's affirmative action program, which was designed to resolve sex-based salary discrimination. It placed the Temple program in a different category than other affirmative action efforts, saying it would permanently discriminate against males, and therefore violate the Equal Pay Act itself.

Yet, in *Winkes v. Brown University*, 747 F.2d 792 (1984), the court endorsed a 36% pay increase, granted to a female professor tempted by another offer, over the legal objections of a male faculty member in the same department. The man claimed that, due to a consent decree the school had entered into designed to bring more female faculty on board, it was offering the female instructor more solely on the basis of her sex. But the court saw the need for matching outside offers when appropriate, and concluded that the Equal Pay Act did not apply. The decision upholds market factors as a legal reason for salary differentials. In other words, while the equal-pay-for-equal-work language is simple, application of the language has proven to be complex.

RULES OF THE WORLD IN ACADEME

The crux of *Brock v. Georgia Southwestern College*, 765 F.2d 1026 (1985), was the question of how the college justified unequal pay rates for faculty members. The U.S. Court of Appeals for the Eleventh Circuit looked at the necessary elements for a successful salary-inequity suit. First, an employee must show that the school pays a member of the opposite sex more for equal work. The jobs in question must be similar, although they do not have to be identical. The jobs must require equal skill, effort, and responsibility. In addition, it is the *jobs*, not the *employees* holding the jobs, that are compared by the court.

Following this review process in *Brock*, the court found that teaching different courses, by itself, does not justify different salaries. Almost all teachers in higher education teach different topics, and this difference cannot explain pay differences. Of the four accepted justifications for pay differences for equal work — seniority, merit, quantity/quality, or sex-neutral factors — Georgia Southwestern argued seniority and merit; but the court found no proof of either. In fact, the court found no legally justifiable reason for the lesser pay rate for females, and thus awarded damages.

Damages in cases like this can be substantial. Where the court finds violations of the Equal Pay Act, it can order payment of two years' back pay, interest, and legal fees. If the court finds the inequity was willful, damages can be at least three years' back pay. The Equal Employment Opportunity Commission (EEOC) has the responsibility to enforce the Act, and provides assistance to employees with causes of action.

The University of Connecticut completed an equal-pay study of its seven campuses, and concluded that sex discrimination is part of the reason for lower salary rates for female instructors. The system has now developed a plan, which has the support of campus bargaining units, to adjust the pay rates of female faculty over two years, and to increase wages for both men and women in traditionally female jobs — such as nursing and library work.

Connecticut's voluntary pay-equity agreement was not the direct result of litigation. However, one interest-group representative noted that the agreement "(shows) academe that the rules of the world apply." And the rules of the world are simple: equal pay for equal work, on and off campus.

Employees Can Speak Out – and They Can't

An Auburn University professor got the word from a federal court: He had no constitutional right to help author a report critical of his department chairman. The court said the First Amendment did not extend to a departmental self-study, because it was not a "matter of public concern." The decision overturned a jury verdict in the mechanical engineering professor's favor. The jury had found that the school improperly transferred him to another department in retaliation for the critical report.

At the University of Central Florida, a teacher sued the board of regents and university officials, charging the school denied him tenure because of his complaints about cheating students. The associate professor of finance spoke out about "rampant" cheating, saying the administration failed to take steps to solve the problem. His lawsuit contended the tenure denial followed as a direct result.

CHILLING THE FREE PLAY OF THE SPIRIT

Decades ago, the issue of what right public university faculty and staff have to criticize their own institutions appeared decided. In the courts' view, public employees agreed to suspend their constitutional rights in exchange for an employment contract. In other words, you had a right to free speech but not a right to a job. It wasn't until the loyalty-oath and organizational-affiliation cases in the 1950s and '60s that the constitutional free speech protections granted others were extended to public employees, including university professors.

In *Shelton v. Tucker*, 364 U.S. 479 (1960), one of the organizational-affiliation cases, the U.S. Supreme Court ruled that "unwarranted inhibition upon the free spirit of teachers ... has an unmistakable tendency to chill that free play of the spirit which all teachers ought especially to cultivate and practice; it makes for caution and timidity in their associations by potential teachers." The decision thus curtailed employers' power to limit employees' speech and outside-of-work activities. Once the courts opened their doors to employer-employee free speech disputes, the flood began – and continues to this day.

Another early case – *Pickering v. Board of Education*, 391 U.S. 563 (1968) – defined the right of instructors to criticize their employers. A high school teacher, fired for writing a letter to a local newspaper critical of the school board, charged the firing violated his constitutional rights. As a citizen, he could write a letter to the paper on any subject he wanted! The Court (not agreeing wholly with that statement) ruled in his favor: Teachers retain the right to comment on matters of public concern, as do all other citizens.

The Court saw a need to balance "the interests of the teacher, as a citizen, in commenting on matters of public concern" against "the interests of the state, as an employer, in promoting the efficiency of the public services it performs through its employees." It held the teacher's comments (concerning financial plans) were of a public, not personal, nature – thus deserving constitutional protection. His concerns did not relate to working conditions, but the future of the school system in general.

WHAT'S PROTECTED?

This case and others established a balancing principle that extended some free speech protections to instructors; but the courts have since kept busy trying to determine what kinds of comments are protected. Defining what "matters of public concern" includes has proven elusive. At one end of the scale, the courts have held mere "academic bickering" has no constitutional protection. Similarly, a finding of no or limited public concern has led to dismissal of constitutional cases involving course syllabi (*Ballard v. Blount*, 734 F.2d 1980), appointments of supervisors (*Montgomery v. Boshears*, 698 F.2d 739), complaints about particular courses (*Landrum v. Eastern Kentucky University*, 578 F.Supp. 241, 247) and skills of a dean (*Pressman v. University of North Carolina at Charlotte*, 337 S.E.2d 644).

A librarian who objected to West Liberty State College's (West Virginia) plans for a new facility was fired, setting the stage for *Orr v. Crowder*, 315 S.E.2d 593 (1984). Her objections to the new building's design led to several confrontations, and eventually the school offered her a final one-year contract. The court agreed with her that the library plans were a matter of public concern, and held that she had the right as a citizen to speak out on the issue. The court balanced her right to speak against the school's need for orderly administration — and found her comments to be protected.

The principles courts apply in reviewing employees' speech critical of employers appear in sharp relief in *Connick v. Meyers*, 461 U.S. 138 (1983). The Court defined "matters of public concern" as those "relating to any matter of political, social, or other concern in the community." Generally, courts find conditions of employment to be "personal," not public matters of concern — and therefore not entitled to First Amendment protections.

Connick centered on a questionnaire which an employee distributed in her office. It questioned office morale, confidence in supervisors, and the need for a grievance committee. The Court held her termination in response to the survey justified as a response to insubordination. Her questionnaire did not concern a matter of public policy, but was more personal in nature. A key feature of the decision is the Court's emphasis on an employer's need for close working relationships, personal loyalty, and confidence in employees.

The courts have tended to give great weight to employers' decisions on employee free speech, because employers must maintain some control over employee conduct. The closer the speaker stands to the object of the criticism, organizationally, the greater the emphasis courts will place on this factor. Put another way, courts are more willing to listen to complaints of disruption (due to the criticism) from co-workers than from more distant administrators, such as presidents or trustees. The test is loyalty and the need for a good working relationship.

In contrast to *Connick*, a professor's right to speak simply as a private citizen was the issue in *Starsky v. Williams*, 353 F.Supp. 900 (1972). An Arizona State University professor went before television cameras and issued a press release to criticize the state board of trustees. In reinstating him to his teaching position after the school fired him for his comments, the court wrote:

"In each of these communications, plaintiff spoke or wrote as a private citizen on a public issue, and in a place and context apart from his role as faculty member. In none ... did he appear as a public spokesman for the university, or claim any kind of expertise related to his profession. He spoke as any citizen might speak, and the board was, therefore, subject to its own avowed standard that when a faculty member 'speaks or writes as a citizen, he should be free from institutional censorship or discipline.' "

Higher education is a special working environment: Courts have noted that faculty members should have more free speech latitude than other types of governmental employees. In an academic environment, "suppression of speech or opinion cannot be justified by an undifferentiated fear or apprehension of disturbance, nor by the mere desire to avoid the discomfort and unpleasantness that always accompany an unpopular viewpoint." *Trotman v. Board of Trustees of Lincoln University*, 635 A.2d 216 (1980).

The Supreme Court's decision in *Rankin v. McPherson*, 107 S.Ct. 2891 (1987), illustrates the principles of *Starsky* and *Trotman*. In that Texas case, the Court ruled that a public employer cannot fire an employee solely in retaliation for engaging in protected expression. The employer must be able to demonstrate a disruptive effect. In *Rankin*, a clerical employee of a police department, upon hearing a report that someone had shot at

President Reagan, remarked, "If they go for him again, I hope they get him." She was fired immediately. The Court took note of the facts that the employer made no inquiry of the remark's effect, if any, on office functions, nor of the speaker's motivation. (Obviously, if the statement had contained a threat, the situation would be different.)

A federal court found a faculty member's concerns over academic integrity protected in *Johnson v. Lincoln University*, 776 F.2d 443 (1985). A chemistry professor wrote to an accrediting agency criticizing the school's academic standards and alleging grade inflation. The university responded by terminating him from a tenured position for insubordination.

A trial court found the professor's concerns to be only personal in nature, but the appellate court held that overall academic integrity is of sufficient public interest to warrant First Amendment protection. Thus, the school couldn't justify retaliatory action.

As we have seen, constitutional free speech protections extend to public-institution faculty and staff members on matters of *public interest*. At issue in the Auburn and Central Florida cases was the exact definition of this term. Complaining employees must show that their speech fits that definition, and that any school action against them resulted from exercising that right. While the school's need for efficiency and loyalty may be at issue in some cases, courts have not treated these as overriding factors in higher education cases. The courts want employees to be free to speak out on issues of public concern, but agree that employers have the right to limit speech of a more personal nature.

What's Behind Employment Discrimination Lawsuits

In 1974, a federal court wrote: "Of all the fields which the federal courts should hesitate to invade and take over, education and faculty appointments at a university level are probably the least suited for federal court." (*Faro v. New York University*, 502 F.2d 1229.) That may still be true, but the fact is discrimination lawsuits against colleges and universities involving employment issues are increasingly visible in the courts today. Hiring, tenure, and termination practices in higher education are subject to court review on a regular basis, despite *Faro*. Campus decisions that a decade or two ago would have been left as campus decisions, are now often settled in court.

Recent statistics, however, show that colleges are upheld in almost four out of five of faculty and staff challenges filed. Even with such limited success, academic employment discrimination cases have created and decided a number of issues that schools (under general threat of suit) should be aware of in developing policies and making employment decisions.

A key issue in any review of discrimination lawsuits — a confused lot at this point — is the right to prevent disclosure of confidential documents used in faculty employment reviews. These records are traditionally cloaked in full "academic freedom," protected from outside review or release. However, some courts have recently allowed limited access to records previously thought sacrosanct. Peer evaluations, made in confidence, were suddenly released for review. Federal appeals courts have split on the issue, and the U.S. Supreme Court turned down a 1986 request for review:

In deciding not to hear an appeal of *Equal Employment Opportunity Commission v. Franklin and Marshall College*, 775 F.2d 110, the high court has permitted different interpretations of the law in different sections of the country. The decision was in favor of

EEOC, allowing the commission access to peer evaluations to review a faculty member's claim of discrimination. Schools attempting to maintain confidentiality of such records must be prepared to show that the institution's interest in keeping the records confidential outweighs the faculty's right to be free from discrimination.

SUBJECTIVE STANDARD?

The idea that tenure can require a level of performance above mere qualification has been tested, and found support, in at least one federal appeals court. In *Namenworth v. Board of Regents, University of Wisconsin*, 769 F.2d 1235, the court ruled that schools may make tenure decisions more subjectively than other employment decisions. This subjective standard has not achieved universal acceptance by the courts; many maintain the need for more objective standards to judge discrimination claims.

There are, of course, legitimate reasons (beyond teaching, research, and publications review) for denying tenure. When faced with charges of unlawful discrimination, colleges should be able to show that such non-discriminatory reasons were in fact the cause of the denial or other employment action. In recent years, such causes as publication in religious, not academic, journals; profanity in the classroom; and poor interpersonal skills have passed muster with the courts, in the face of a discrimination charge, to support decisions not to hire or promote.

Language of faculty contracts and handbooks may also establish grounds for discrimination suits. University affirmative action policies arguably create an employment contract, and can be cited in support of a legal challenge.

Higher education discrimination law comes from a variety of sources, both federal and state. The Fourteenth Amendment to the Constitution and Title VII of the Civil Rights Act of 1964 are the standard sources for employees' protection from discrimination. In addition to federal statutes and standards, many states have adopted similar laws to provide even greater protection for employees.

The "equal protection of the laws" language of the Fourteenth Amendment was long held to bar governmental race discrimination. Only in the last two decades has the clause been judicially expanded to bar sex-based discrimination as well — unless a strong governmental interest exists supporting the need for sex-based classifications.

Most legal challenges against colleges and universities do not rely solely on the Equal Protection clause, for several reasons. First, the language applies only to "state action," putting private schools out of its reach. Second, monetary awards in discrimination actions tend to be bigger when other statutes are cited.

Finally, in order to successfully sue under the Equal Protection clause, a plaintiff must show that, not only was there discrimination, but there was an intent on the part of the institution to unlawfully discriminate.

Title VII of the Civil Rights Act of 1964 is more often the tool of choice when challenging institutions' hiring or promotion policies. The Act prohibits employment policies discriminatory as to race, color, religion, sex, or national origin. The law originally allowed an exemption for academic institutions "with respect to the employment of individuals to perform work connected with the educational activities" of the school. That exception died in 1972.

Attempts by some schools to escape coverage through affiliation with the state or a church have generally failed. An effort to remain exempt under the doctrine of sovereign immunity was shot down in *Shawer v. Indiana University of Pennsylvania*, 602 F.2d 1161 (1979); separation of church and state was found not to limit discrimination liability in *EEOC v. Mississippi College*, 626 F.2d 477 (1980).

In order to pursue an allegation of discrimination under Title VII, a plaintiff must follow a process first set out in *McDonnell Douglas Corp. v. Green*, 411 U.S. 792 (1973).

Plaintiffs must first show that they:

- are members of a protected class;
- applied for and were qualified for a position the employer wanted to fill;
- were rejected despite their qualifications; and
- the position remained open while the employer continued the search.

If a would-be college employee establishes these things, the burden shifts to the institution — which must, at this point, be able to provide a non-discriminatory reason for not offering the plaintiff the position or promotion. If the employer is able to provide a proper rebuttal to the allegations, the burden shifts back to the plaintiff, who has one more opportunity to show that unlawful discrimination was the basis for the institution's action.

Faculty and staff discrimination suits, based on federal and state laws as well as on contractual obligations, are increasing. Awareness on the part of colleges and universities of the bases for these suits, and the issues they raise, is necessary to provide a truly fair employment opportunity for all — and to help prevent many future lawsuits.

Principles

- Have written and well-publicized policies defining and prohibiting sexual harassment, as well as a system of resolving complaints.

- All the questions you should avoid in candidate interviews — about past discrimination charges, credit problems, mental problems, child care, spouse's approval, or religion — are also off limits for reference checks.

- Always depend on facts for responses in giving references; make no guesses.

- There are two distinct sets of rules for campus collective bargaining. While the NLRB has asserted jurisdiction over private schools and their faculty, public post-secondary education is exempt from federal labor relations laws, and subject only to state authority.

- If there are pay differences between the sexes at your institution, know the reason. Not having a reason (even if there is no conscious effort to discriminate) may mean losing an equal-pay lawsuit.

- Teachers retain the right to comment on matters of public concern, as do all other citizens.

- When faced with charges of unlawful discrimination, colleges should be able to show that non-discriminatory reasons were in fact the cause of the denial or other employment action.

8. Justice on Campus

The misconduct hearing was held on March 24, 1980, as scheduled; and Kusnir appeared with his brother, who acted as his advisor in the proceedings. On March 25, 1980, the Conduct Board found that Kusnir was a culpable participant in the misconduct charged. That determination, in addition to the fact that Kusnir was already on disciplinary probation for fighting, induced the Conduct Board to recommend his suspension: for the balance of that academic year and the Fall semester of 1980. From that decision Kusnir appealed to the College president challenging the propriety of his suspension. In that challenge Kusnir asserted that the College had no jurisdiction over the off-campus incident. He also asserted that he had been deprived of due process in that he was (1) not adequately informed of the charges against him; (2) not advised of his right to legal counsel; and (3) not given an opportunity to appear and "prepare" a defense.

On April 2, 1980, the College president dismissed the appeal and entered a written decision adopting the suspension recommendation.

On May 2, 1980, Kusnir filed his Petition for Review with this Court. Companion to the instant appeal, he requested this Court to stay his suspension pending disposition of the case. On May 5, 1980, this Court entered an order staying the suspension; but only to the extent of allowing Appellant Kusnir to complete his then current school term, the Spring semester of 1980. In short, the Appellant's period of suspension from school would be coextensive with the Fall semester of 1980.

The College and its president, as the named respondents in this matter, initially sought to challenge Kusnir's appeal to this Court by preliminary objections. When those objections were overruled, the respondents filed a motion under Pa.R.A.P. 1972 to transfer the case to the Board of Claims. That motion was directed to be heard at the same time as argument on the merits of the appeal.

We consider first the transfer motion ...
— *Kusnir v. Leach*, 439 A.2d at 225 (1982)

All of this brouhaha over a crashed off-campus party. Ah, for the good old days!

With this chapter we come full circle; we'll be seeing some of the due process principles from Chapter 1 argued in action. *Kusnir* raises one specific issue we address in detail: the "right" of students to be represented (or is it advised?) at campus disciplinary hearings.

We look here at how to evaluate your present campus judicial system; possibilities for planning a new or revised dispute-resolution system; the law of reporting crimes committed by students; taking care of on-campus discipline when students are also charged with criminal violations; and a study of that modern phenomenon, the lawyer in the campus disciplinary hearing.

Reporting Students' Crime

"Do I have to report a crime if I see one being committed, or know one took place?" This is a question which student leaders and college administrators are sometimes in the uncomfortable position of having to ask. The legal obligation to report criminal activity on campus is not always clear. Responsibility varies with circumstances.

Several states' and federal statutes make it a crime *not to report information* about a felony. Typical state-statute language reads, "No person, knowing that a felony has been committed, shall knowingly fail to report such information to law enforcement agencies."

In common law, the phrase "misprision of felony" refers to the concept which would make the failure to report a crime a crime in itself. The original duty to report crimes came in the days when there was no professional law enforcement and citizen reports were the only source of crime control. Anyone with knowledge of a crime was responsible for alerting the rest of the community.

In some states, the crime of misprision of felony remains on the books. These laws state that a person is criminally negligent if he fails to stop a felony from taking place, or fails to help bring the offender to justice after the crime.

Federal misprision of felony law (U.S. Code, Title 18, Section 4) applies to a person "having knowledge of the actual commission of a felony ... (who) conceals and does not as soon as possible make known, the same" to law enforcement or judicial officers. Violation carries a $500 fine, up to three years in prison, or both.

The trend in recent times has been away from the general application of misprision of felony. However, even in those states without specific misprision of felony laws, those who know of, but don't report, a felony are at risk. Here's where two common TV-cop phrases come into play — accessory after the fact," and "aiding and abetting." These laws typically apply to persons *unrelated* to the felon, who fail to report the felonious activity.

Be *very* careful when dealing with situations where a felony may have been committed. It's not always possible to promise a student or staff member that, as part of an arrangement, the crime will not be reported. Be knowledgeable about the laws in your state concerning misprision of felony and accessory after the fact. Don't add to an already complicated and difficult situation by leaving yourself open to prosecution for failing to report a crime when required to do so.

Obstruction of justice must also be considered by school officials, when they take steps to handle campus misconduct that is also technically a crime. Common-law legal sources indicate that it constitutes an obstruction of justice to do any act which prevents, obstructs, impedes, or hinders the due course of public justice. Care must be taken to avoid acts that could be considered obstruction — for example, confiscating a small quantity of drugs from a student, destroying it, and then beginning campus disciplinary proceedings. In such a case, public law-enforcement officials could take action against the administrators for obstructing justice through the destruction of evidence. Willful destruction of evidence or concealment of what someone knows will likely be evidence in a criminal case and would be prosecutable. It is no defense that the evidence has not yet been sought by search warrant or subpoena. However, in cases where there is little likelihood that criminal charges will be filed, and the extent of the evidence lost is limited, criminal charges against an administrator would not be successful where there is no shown intent to frustrate the law.

Failure to report a crime or take action can be a crime under circumstances where a special duty exists or is imposed by law. As an example, there is a general duty of all persons to report cases of suspected child abuse and neglect. Public employees at state colleges may also have a legal duty to report crimes involving state property. This duty could include cases of suspected arson, theft, embezzlement, or misuse of state equipment and facilities. Other examples of duty to report crimes include motor vehicle accident reports, reports to medical examiners, and some health reports.

As with most things, the best policy to follow when faced with questions involving a duty to report crimes is a policy well thought out in advance. Duty to report crimes and obstruction of justice should always be seriously considered when dealing with criminal activity as an on-campus disciplinary matter.

Disciplining Students in Trouble with the Law

Sure, a college or university has the authority to discipline its own students.

But what about those students who, on top of subjecting themselves to campus disciplinary measures, have gotten on the wrong side of the law? How and when does the institution handle this?

The University of Texas was ordered to wait until the end of criminal proceedings before holding a campus hearing for students arrested in an anti-apartheid demonstration. A state judge ruled that requiring students to participate in campus proceedings before their criminal cases are decided would place them in "an awkward position."

But institutions can find themselves in just as awkward a position attempting to handle disciplinary cases when there is a criminal trial pending. The general legal trend has been to uphold the school's authority to discipline students who are also the subjects of off-campus proceedings. (The often-misunderstood principle of double jeopardy does not apply to these situations, because the campus proceedings are not criminal law proceedings, and because their purpose is not punitive.)

NO NEED TO WAIT?

A large body of case law permits schools to hold student disciplinary hearings before criminal cases are tried or decided, including *Nzuve v. Castleton State College*, 335 A.2d 321, and *Hart v. Ferris State College*, 557 F.Supp. 1379. These cases have held that a student's due process rights are not violated when a campus hearing takes place before off-campus charges are settled.

In *Nzuve*, the college was attempting to discipline a student accused of burglary, assault, and rape. By waiting until the disposition of criminal charges, the court noted, the school might allow some students to complete their educations in the meantime, "effectively completing an 'end run' around the disciplinary rules and procedures" of the school. The court concluded: "Educational institutions have both a need and a right to formulate their own standards and enforce them."

Hart involved the sale of illegal drugs and an off-campus arrest of a student. The school discipline procedures included extensive due process protections, but the student argued that the court should bar campus proceedings until completion of the criminal case. The court permitted both the campus and criminal cases to continue at the same time.

FIFTH AMENDMENT CONCERNS

The Constitution guarantees that no one "shall be compelled in any criminal case to be a witness against himself." How does a decision like the one in *Hart* square with this guarantee? In campus disciplinary proceedings, when a student is required to testify or the failure to testify will be held against her, testimony she gives cannot be used in later criminal proceedings (*Furutani v. Ewigleben*, 87 S.Ct. 616). However, if a student is not compelled to testify, and failure to testify will not be held against her, any testimony the student gives on campus is considered voluntary. Under these conditions, testimony could be used against her in later criminal proceedings (*Gabrilowitz v. Newman*, 582 F.2d 100).

The courts have used this protection from criminal self-incrimination when campus testimony is compelled as a reason to permit colleges to hold prior disciplinary proceedings. The courts have found no violation of students' Fifth Amendment rights.

However, in the recent Texas case, the arrested students successfully argued that prior campus testimony would violate their rights against self-incrimination. According to the students, if they testified, they would lose the opportunity to defend themselves or ask for leniency. This state decision runs contrary to most case law on the issue; schools should consult local counsel before reviewing campus guidelines on the handling of such situations.

The 13 Texas students were arrested for "disruptive activity," a misdemeanor, after locking themselves in the UT president's office during a campus demonstration. The school had planned disciplinary hearings for them after they refused to accept one-year suspensions, but was forced to delay those hearings until the end of the criminal proceedings.

In such a case, if the students are acquitted of criminal charges, the school can still proceed against them, using a lower burden of proof than the "beyond a reasonable doubt" required for criminal conviction. If the students are convicted, the school still must give them a campus hearing prior to any disciplinary action.

Campus Judicial Systems: Take a Look at How They Work

Too often, attention focuses on campus judicial systems only when there is unrest or some other serious problem. But that is exactly the wrong time to be taking a close look at the system's functioning. Judicial systems are necessary elements of today's colleges and universities, and need attention from administrators on a continuing basis. A system of campus justice not regularly evaluated can easily fail when it is needed most. Ongoing formal and informal evaluation methods insure that the system is fair and meets the institution's needs. To be successful, a campus judicial system *must be in sync with the basic philosophy* of the institution — must advance the needs and desires of the institution. In other words, administrators must coordinate a school's judicial philosophy with the overall campus philosophy for the judicial system to be effective.

Before looking at what something does, it is important to understand why it does it in the first place. In recent years, most higher education justice systems have been based on *student development* and *educational* principles. These systems place importance on students' personal growth and development in matters of discipline, rather than seeking purely punitive sanctions. Therefore, when evaluating a campus judicial system, you must first review and understand the mission statements of the school and of the discipline system. Only then can formal and informal evaluations be truly effective.

Organized judicial-system review should contain the following: (1) agreed-upon methods of review; (2) a well-defined scope; and (3) a process for implementing recommendations or making use of conclusions. Remember that working with *all involved constituencies* — faculty, students, and staff — in planning, conducting, and following up on an evaluation process helps insure its effectiveness.

REVIEW METHODS

There is a variety of methods useful in reviewing judicial systems on campus. Among the most common are observations, surveys, required reports, interviews, informal feedback, and review committees. It is impossible to say here which of these methods or what combination of methods is appropriate for given institutions. You should consider these methods and others in developing and planning for a comprehensive judicial-system review tailored to meet your campus' needs.

- *Observations* involve having appropriate staff members attend judicial sessions, and provide reports to evaluators.

- *Surveys* are useful for gathering information on justice systems. They can test the system's impact, collect faculty's, students', and staff's perceptions of the system's procedures and results, and probe sentiments of both victims and violators.

- *Reports* can be required of staff members and students involved in the justice system and sitting on judicial bodies. Review these in order to measure how much use the system gets, and to identify problem areas.

- *Interviews* with involved faculty, students, and staff can be formal or informal. Use these for soliciting information on how the system is working, and what could improve its effectiveness.

- *Information feedback* can come from many sources, and is often unsolicited. Personal reactions of those who participate in judicial proceedings, letters to the student press, and similar feedback can help in assessing the system.

- *Review committees* can conduct formal evaluations, incorporating many of these.

No matter what the chosen method or methods, there are several key questions evaluators must address:

(1) *Does the system properly protect students' rights?*

(2) *Is the system educational rather than punitive, helping modify behaviors while teaching students to accept responsibility for their actions?*

(3) *Does it teach members of the campus community about rights and responsibilities, and give panel members an opportunity for personal development?*

Ask these basic, important questions at each stage of the evaluation process — planning and development, the review itself, and implementation.

SCOPE OF REVIEW

As important as choosing the methods of review is determining *which* system components to review. An ongoing review program can examine individual components regularly, while a comprehensive review can evaluate the entire system at one time. Make sure to review the following components at one time or another, however: publications, training programs, practices and procedures, consistency in sanctions, and personnel.

Keep *publications* and written materials used in the judicial process up-to-date and consistent, to be sure the system is fair and effective from both the institution's and students' perspectives. Consider changes when publications are not serving the twin goals of justice for students and preservation of institutional needs.

Good judicial systems have good *training programs* for members. Evaluate the training process before, during, and after the year. You can measure its effectiveness immediately after training sessions, during the semester, and at year's end through surveys and interviews. The critical requirement: Training programs must adequately prepare judicial board members for their duties.

Examine the *practices and procedures* of judicial boards to make sure they don't violate students' due process rights. Looking at exceptional cases, or cases overturned on appeal, is helpful in evaluating this component. College counsel should also review procedures.

A common complaint about both on- and off-campus judicial systems is lack of *consistency in sanctions.* Review past records periodically, looking for trends or problems.

Personnel are obviously important to judicial systems; include them in your evaluation. Look at both professional staff members involved in judicial affairs, and members of judicial boards. In the case of professional staff, annual performance reviews and regularly scheduled staff meetings are useful in evaluation. Judicial panel members may not be subject to ongoing appraisal, so additional methods — like peer and advisor review — may be necessary.

USING THE RESULTS

Evaluating a campus judicial system for the sake of evaluation is of little or no value, of course. Have a plan in advance for making the best use of results.

Consider the results or conclusions with two things in mind: (1) the institution's needs, and (2) students' rights. An improved judicial system must serve both. Evaluating the system — using proven methods, examining all components, following a plan — is the route to that improvement.

Plan Dispute-Resolution System Carefully

Do your policies regarding complaints cover the expected variety of complaints?

Are the complaint procedures simple to follow?

Is the process effective? Cost-efficient? Timely? Available to students and staff?

Do individual dispute-resolution decisions lead to campus improvements?

The answers to these questions, and others concerning campus dispute-resolution systems, may be very important to your learning environment. Complaints are a normal part of any learning, living, or working situation; therefore, colleges and universities must be prepared to deal effectively with complaints from students, faculty, and staff.

One key to staying out of court is *a system of appropriate response* to complaints. If, through informal or formal conflict-resolution techniques, a problem can be solved on campus, the major problems caused by legal action — morale, productivity, time, and expense — can be avoided. Administrators should place a high priority on campus resolution of campus problems.

ALTERNATIVE MEANS

In recent years, on college campuses and elsewhere, there has been a trend toward the development of *alternative means of conflict resolution.* Contributing to this trend is the fact that the courts are not prepared to handle the variety and number of cases that come before them — and are therefore unable to resolve all the conflicts those cases entail.

For colleges, this can mean new ways of dealing with employee complaints, or student grievances. The need for swifter settlements; the desire for being less legally encumbered; the opportunity to get to the root of conflicts, not just a result; and convenience of time, location, and structure all encourage the development of alternative dispute-resolution methods. Thus systems involving *mediation and arbitration* are becoming more visible on campuses.

Given the unique nature of higher education institutions, no one plan for handling campus complaints works everywhere. However, many elements of successful, established policies can apply to most situations. In developing dispute-resolution policies, institutions should keep two goals in mind: resolving complaints fairly; and resolving them as quickly as

possible. In addition, complaint-resolution procedures should:
- be comprehensive
- allow for some flexibility
- allow for a full and fair hearing of the issues
- establish a system to identify problem areas — in order to avoid further, similar difficulties.

The *size* of the school is also an important factor in determining the proper problem-resolution system. Small schools may emphasize informal processes and limited involvement of neutral third parties. At a larger school, the complexity of administration and chains of command may dictate more formal procedures. The actual elements of the process may not differ; but the emphasis a school places on specific elements can vary greatly.

The need for *comprehensiveness* is based on the wide range of problems that are encountered on campus, and the complexity of the issues. A single complaint can involve many campus units, policies, and procedures. If a dispute-resolution system is to be effective, it must respond directly to all issues in need of resolution. Of course, a school can have different resolution processes for different issues or problems; but remember, the greater the number of systems, the greater the opportunity for confusion and duplication. Therefore, systems should be comprehensive, but as straightforward and simple as possible.

BE FLEXIBLE

The need for *flexibility* in the process, based on the highly varied environment of a college campus, is a driving force behind *informal* resolution procedures, such as mediation. Administrators must do all they can to promote problem resolution *before* complaints are filed. Informal procedures can be more expedient and more effective — few outside parties are drawn into the process. As anyone who has ever tried to mediate a dispute knows, the best opportunity to resolve a problem is at the earliest opportunity.

Mediation uses an uninvolved third party to work out a solution to a dispute. The goal is for the mediator to *assist* in finding a mutually acceptable resolution. Appropriate for faculty-staff complaint mediation are items such as class scheduling, teaching assignments, and allocation of office and research space.

Mediation is a process of discussion, clarification, and compromise. Voluntary settlement, as opposed to an imposed settlement, is the objective. A mediator generally has *no enforcement powers*; he depends entirely on his skill, and on strategies designed to promote solutions. Mediators can also address some common student problems such as roommate disputes, landlord-tenant wars, and fraternity conflicts.

These kinds of issues may not end up in court if they go unresolved, but failure to deal with them may create a campus environment where other, more serious matters are difficult to deal with. Even tenure-related issues can be dealt with through mediation. While not appropriate for tenure decisions themselves, a well-run dispute-mediation system can *limit the issues* in tenure disputes. With side issues out of the way, greater focus is possible elsewhere, on the most important issues in the decision.

The need for a *full and impartial hearing* as part of dispute-resolution may be obvious — but deserves emphasis. Students, faculty, and staff must know that their concerns will see a fair hearing by an unbiased hearing officer or committee. There are several reasons this is important: (1) to develop a full record of the complaint and evidence; (2) to allow for review of all arguments; and (3) to establish an understanding that the system is open and fair to all.

Also important for improved dispute-resolution systems is the *ability to identify problem areas and make improvements*, to prevent future difficulties of the same nature. If a system is designed to address only the concerns of the parties, little or no thought will go into the overall needs of the campus community. To address the community's future needs, not only the parties' current needs, the system should be set up to examine the *reasons* for problems, and recommend changes in policies or practices to improve the campus environment.

The trend toward mediation and arbitration in higher education disputes appears to be accelerating. Institutions — and individuals — who wish to avoid the obstacles and expense of drawn-out legal maneuvers are looking more to external-review systems to swiftly resolve differences. Many campuses still view mediation and arbitration as unnecessary outside interference in their spheres of governance; but the high cost of, and dissatisfaction with, current legal process has begun to change more than a few minds.

Well-developed dispute-resolution systems can *decrease* the number of lawsuits and the amount of governmental interference on campuses, despite fears that mediation causes colleges to "lose control." In fact, it is disputes that go all the way to court that spell significant loss of control by the parties. Judges and juries are not always familiar with higher education practices, traditions, and needs. The adversarial legal process may not be the best tool with which to develop lasting, equitable solutions.

Arbitration, in which the third party wields more authority than in mediation, nevertheless allows the parties to retain significant control over the process. Arbitrators can be selected to represent the parties' needs and concerns; ground rules can be established to factor in financial conditions, levels of authority, and timetables for decision-making. Arbitration can, in fact, be more cost-effective and provide better dispute resolution than mediation.

Student, faculty, and staff complaints at colleges and universities have to be handled in a fair and timely manner. Perhaps the time has come for mediation and arbitration to come into their own, as legitimate alternatives to lengthy, costly, confusing, unsatisfying courtroom battles.

For more information on the mediation process, contact: University of Massachusetts Mediation Project, 127 Hasbrouck Hall, University of Massachusetts, Amherst, MA 01003.

When Lawyers Invade the Campus Hearing

The University of Vermont student, in a variation of the classic "crib notes," had a "handful" of history exam answers. That is, they were written on his hand. Suspended by the university after conviction in a campus disciplinary hearing, he offered the latest challenge to rules prohibiting students from retaining attorneys. The student claimed his due process constitutional rights were violated by UVM's refusal to allow an attorney to speak for him during the hearing, and wanted the federal court in Burlington to overturn the suspension.

In the last two decades, institutions' rules about the *presence* of and *role* of attorneys in campus judicial proceedings have been the subject of many court challenges. Do students have the right to have counsel present for hearings? Do they have any right to legal representation at all? If so, what can the attorney do — can she argue the student's case?

Case law has produced clear answers. Students have no absolute right to be represented by legal counsel in campus proceedings. Colleges can prohibit or limit the role of attorneys in most circumstances.

HOW MUCH PROCESS IS DUE?

As with much higher education due process law, many leading decisions in this area came out of the campus unrest of the late 1960s. A football game at Bluefield State College (West Virginia) was the site of one student demonstration. Students facing campus charges growing out of the incident were suspended after they refused to participate in disciplinary proceedings without a lawyer. The Sixth Amendment — right to counsel in criminal cases — was the basis of their challenge to the suspension. The court ruled that the Sixth Amendment's guarantee does not extend to *civil* matters. It held the school had discretion to establish rules on the role of legal counsel in campus proceedings. Bluefield need only *enforce* the rules fairly. (*Barker v. Hardway*, 283 F.Supp. 228 (1968).)

Proceeding on a different basis — the Fourteenth Amendment's guarantee of due process — another group of student protesters had their claim of absolute right to counsel shot down in *Haynes v. Dallas County Junior College District*, 386 F.Supp. 208 (1974). The protest did not break up when ordered by administrators. The school brought charges against several students, and ultimately suspended them. The suspendees challenged the decision, but the court concluded the campus' policy of no lawyers was reasonable, and that the due process clause does not require that lawyers be allowed in disciplinary proceedings.

When it comes to academic dishonesty, courts give great latitude to the institution. They are notoriously reluctant to involve themselves in grades and degrees, and that reluctance carries over to academic dishonesty proceedings. In *Garshman v. Pennsylvania State University*, 395 F.Supp. 912 (1975), a first-year medical student was charged with cheating on exams. The university limited representation during campus proceedings to an advisor from the academic community. That advisor was not limited in his role, but outside legal counsel was prohibited.

Challenged in federal court, the university prevailed. Noting the widely held belief among judges that judges should not become involved in academic decision-making, the court concluded that "a determination as to the academic honesty of a student is analogous to the determination of professional competency of a professor and is a matter peculiarly within the discretion of a college administration."

In short, as long as an institution can show basic fairness in its process, there is no general right to counsel for academic proceedings.

TWO CASES WHERE THEY'RE IN

There are situations in which lawyers are necessary for *fairness*. The courts have spelled out two of these: First, when a student faces serious charges on *and* off campus, he has the right to have counsel present during the campus proceedings, to protect his rights off campus. Second, when schools use attorneys to prosecute students in disciplinary and academic dishonesty cases, the students must have access to counsel.

In *Gabrilowitz v. Newman*, 582 F.2d 100 (1978), the First Circuit U.S. Court of Appeals dealt with the case of a University of Rhode Island student accused of assault with intent to rape. The student faced similar charges off campus, but was denied legal representation by the school for the campus proceedings. As in *Garshman*, university rules allowed only representation by an advisor of the student's choice from within the university community. The accused student demanded legal counsel on campus, on the ground that his testimony on campus could be used against him off campus, and went to federal court to get it.

The district court judge agreed: When facing similar, serious charges off campus, a college student has the right to have a lawyer present on campus to protect against self-incrimination. The university appealed. The First Circuit upheld the decision, in an opinion which provides important guidance on the *role* of lawyers in campus proceedings:

First, the court noted that any voluntary student testimony at a campus hearing is admissible in a later off-campus criminal case. Because of this, legal counsel is necessary on campus for a student facing outside charges. *However*, that doesn't mean the student's attorney can take an unlimited part in the campus drama; the court ruled that the attorney under these circumstances is there to *protect the student's interests, not affect the outcome*. Put another way, the school may limit the role of counsel to that of an advisor. Observation of the proceedings, and giving of advice, is sufficient protection for the student's criminal rights. Full participation, or for that matter, partial participation by the attorney is not necessary to safeguard those rights.

Fairness dictates that when the school has attorneys at the hearing, so must the students. The late-'60s case of *French v. Bashful*, 303 F.Supp. 1333 (1969), illustrates this. Student protesters at Southern University (Louisiana) faced senior law students prosecuting the school's case. The students claimed they were at a legal disadvantage because they were denied counsel. The court agreed, ruling that although there is no general right to an attorney, sometimes one is needed to promote basic fairness.

Finally, *state law* may require counsel in some public-institution hearings. Such was the case in *Kusnir v. Leach*, 439 A.2d 223 (1982). In that Pennsylvania case, the court took care to point out that the students' right to counsel did not derive from the Constitution — rather, it was a creature of state legislation, which the court interpreted to establish the right in proceedings against students at state schools.

Who chooses the student's attorney in cases where the student is entitled to one? *McLaughlin v. Massachusetts Maritime Academy*, 564 F.Supp. 809 (1983), settled that question. A student at the military school was charged with a serious drug offense. The academy wanted to limit his choice of counsel to military personnel; the student wanted a civilian lawyer. The court agreed with the student, ruling that denial of choice of counsel is a violation of due process. Thus, when legal representation is called for, the choice belongs to the student, not the school.

CONCLUSION

The most recent test of campus rules against attorneys came out of the same court that decided *Gabrilowitz*. In *Gorman v. University of Rhode Island*, 837 F.2d 7 (1988), the First Circuit U.S. Court of Appeals reaffirmed the basic principles concerning right to counsel in campus proceedings. *Fairness does not require a lawyer*, unless the school uses one to prosecute cases, or a student faces serious and similar charges on and off campus.

The courts have consistently ruled that:

(1) there is no absolute constitutional right to an attorney in campus proceedings;

(2) the Sixth Amendment's right to counsel in criminal cases does not extend to civil matters, including college disciplinary and academic dishonesty proceedings;

(3) the right to legal representation is limited to situations where schools use attorneys to prosecute cases, or where a lawyer is necessary to protect the student's Fifth Amendment rights (against compelled self-incrimination) because of pending criminal charges off campus; and

(4) when a lawyer is required, her role may be limited to supplying advice to the student.

In the end, constitutional due process is no more than fairness, and the courts have decreed that fairness is possible without lawyers. Put in slightly more adversarial terms, fairness is possible without the insertion of an outsider into a campus community matter — if that is what the school administration thinks best.

Principles

- Duty to report crimes and obstruction of justice should always be seriously considered when dealing with criminal activity as an on-campus disciplinary matter.

- In general, schools may hold student disciplinary hearings before related criminal cases are tried or decided.

- When evaluating a campus judicial system, you must first review and understand the mission statements of the school and of the discipline system.

- Informal dispute-resolution procedures can be more expedient and more effective — few outside parties are drawn into the process.

- The due process clause of the Constitution does not require that lawyers be allowed in disciplinary proceedings.

- When facing similar, serious charges off campus, a college student has the right to have a lawyer present on campus to protect against self-incrimination.

- Fairness dictates that when the school has an attorney at a disciplinary hearing, so must the student.

The articles included in *PERSPECTIVES AND PRINCIPLES: A College Administrator's Guide to Staying Out of Court* were selected and updated from information which first appeared in *PERSPECTIVE: The Campus Legal Monthly* — a newsletter dedicated to helping campus administrators prevent unnecessary loss, injury, and lawsuits, by keeping them legally informed. For a **free review issue** of *PERSPECTIVE*, write: Magna Publications, 2718 Dryden Drive, Madison, WI 53704, or call **1-800-433-0499** (608-249-2455 in Wisconsin).

ALSO AVAILABLE FROM MAGNA PUBLICATIONS:

Newsletters
National On-Campus Report
Academic Leader
Administrator: The Management Newsletter for Higher Education
Recruitment and Retention in Higher Education
The Teaching Professor

Resources
16 Legal Nightmares in Higher Education
by Dennis R. Black, Esq.

The Complete Telemarketing Handbook for Recruiting and Retaining Students
by Anthony V. Pappas, Jr., Ph.D.

How Am I Teaching? Forms and Activities for Acquiring Instructional Input
by Maryellen Weimer, Ph.D., Joan L. Parrett, Ph.D., and Mary-Margaret Kerns, M.S.

Developing Academic Leaders:
Guidelines for Conducting Leadership Workshops and Seminars
by Allan Tucker, Ph.D.

Suicide on Campus: Caring and Coping
by Nancy O'Malley

Notes and Comments on Leadership
Off The Cuff: Tips on How to Survive in a Bureaucracy
Three Keys to Working Effectively with Committees
Great Ideas in Higher Education Management: The Best of Administrator
34 Ideas You Can Use From National On-Campus Report
Making Changes: 27 Strategies from Recruitment and Retention in Higher Education